# ATLAS
# POETICA

*A Journal of Poetry of Place
in Contemporary Tanka*

## Number 19     Autumn, 2014

M. Kei, editor
Amora Johnson, technical director
Yancy Carpentier, editorial assistant
toki, proofreader

2014
Keibooks, Perryville, Maryland, USA

# KEIBOOKS

P O Box 516
Perryville, Maryland, USA 21903
AtlasPoetica.org Editor@AtlasPoetica.org

*Atlas Poetica*
*A Journal of Poetry of Place in Contemporary Tanka*

Atlas Poetica : A Journal of Poetry of Place in Contemporary Tanka, a triannual print and e-journal, is dedicated to publishing and promoting fine poetry of place in modern English tanka (including variant forms). *Atlas Poetica* is interested in both traditional and innovative verse of high quality and in all serious attempts to assimilate the best of the Japanese waka/tanka/kyoka/gogyoshi genres into a continuously developing English short verse tradition. In addition to verse, *Atlas Poetica* publishes articles, essays, reviews, interviews, letters to the editor, etc., related to tanka poetry of place. Tanka in translation from around the world are welcome in the journal.

Published by Keibooks


ISBN 978-0692308042 (Print)
AtlasPoetica.org

# TABLE OF CONTENTS

# Educational Use Notice

Keibooks of Perryville, Maryland, USA, publisher of the journal, *Atlas Poetica : A Journal of Poetry of Place in Contemporary Tanka*, is dedicated to tanka education in schools and colleges, at every level. It is our intention and our policy to facilitate the use of *Atlas Poetica* and related materials to the maximum extent feasible by educators at every level of school and university studies.

Educators, without individually seeking permission from the publisher, may use *Atlas Poetica : A Journal of Poetry of Place in Contemporary Tanka's* online digital editions and print editions as primary or ancillary teaching resources. Copyright law "Fair Use" guidelines and doctrine should be interpreted very liberally with respect to *Atlas Poetica* precisely on the basis of our explicitly stated intention herein. This statement may be cited as an effective permission to use *Atlas Poetica* as a text or resource for studies. Proper attribution of any excerpt to *Atlas Poetica* is required. This statement applies equally to digital resources and print copies of the journal.

Individual copyrights of poets, authors, artists, etc., published in *Atlas Poetica* are their own property and are not meant to be compromised in any way by the journal's liberal policy on "Fair Use." Any educator seeking clarification of our policy for a particular use may email the Editor of *Atlas Poetica* at editor@AtlasPoetica.org. We welcome innovative uses of our resources for tanka education.

Atlas Poetica
Keibooks
P O Box 516
Perryville, MD 21903
<http://AtlasPoetica.org>

# Tanka of South Asia and the Diaspora

This issue's emphasis is on the tanka of South Asia and the Diaspora. It follows our Special Feature online, 'on the cusp of dawn : 25 tanka poets from India' edited by Kala Ramesh.

Poets from Iran to Indonesia and Nepal to Sri Lanka have contributed a wide range of poems. Some of the poets are familiar to us, such as Sonam Chhoki, who writes about her birthplace of Bhutan, but many are new voices, like Payal A. Agarwal, who gives us a glimpse of the life of a working man employed in a food stall in India, while Radhey Shiam, who has occasionally appeared in these pages, gives a charming depiction of a courtship between an admiring young woman and her slightly clueless boyfriend.

Others are voices of the Diaspora, such as Indo-American Grunge who has a thoroughly modern and urban view of life even as he evokes mythological metaphors, and Alex von Vaupel, of Indonesian-Dutch heritage, who struggles with his family legacy of colonialism. We are especially pleased to showcase the work of Indo-Canadian poet Nilufer Y. Mistry, originally from Calcutta, India, but now a resident of British Columbia. Experimenting with form and format, she utilizes space, punctuation, and line breaks to create calligraphy-like images in tanka.

Still other poets are not of South Asian ancestry, but have personal experiences that connect deeply to the region. Michael G. Smith gives a moving account of adopting a daughter from Nepal, but Marilyn Humbert takes us on a nearly mythical trip to the mountains. Many of the travelers come as pilgrims, either accidentally or on purpose. Genie Nakano and Kath Abela Wilson gives us several sequences about India and Iran, and a responsive sequence as well. Richard St. Clair was not able to visit in person, so he takes an imaginary pilgrimage with the Buddha.

Tanka are often used as rose-colored lenses with which to view a romanticized world, but not so Julie B. Cain. She recounts a news report about a mullah in Afganistan who raped a young girl. The 'green peach' is now in danger from her family from the shame she has brought upon them. Samantha Sirimanne Hyde writes about what it is like to be an outsider both at home in Sri Lanka and in her new country of Australia. Verbal bombs, *"go home curry muncher"* remind her of actual bombs, "in that dazing way of karma."

Moving beyond South Asia, Chen-ou Liu gives us a depiction of the exigencies of life in Taiwan as his friend moves through compulsory military service and into the IKEA packaged life of modern Taipei, while Sanford Goldstein muses on many topics from murder to music in his Japanese hometown. Rodney Williams, an Australian, comes as a tourist to the United States and visits Ground Zero and Niagara Falls, while Rebecca Drouilhet writes about the Mississippi River.

On the surface, most of the poems in the issue are gilded and rosy, yet they carry with them ashes of loss. Scenes of beauty and spirituality unfold, but underneath is the uneasy awareness that reality is not so quaint. Wherever they are from and whatever their background, the poets flit back and forth across boundaries that mean so much in terms of politics and possibilities, but do so with the realization that all such borders are arbitrary. Beneath it all we share a common humanity.

We are also able to offer numerous non-fiction book reviews and articles, such as David Rice's discussion of responsive tanka and Peter Fiore's article on tanka prose. All are sure to enhance your enjoyment of tanka literature.

~K~

M. Kei
*Editor, Atlas Poetica*

*Floods at the India–Nepal Border.*

*Cover Image courtesy of Earth Observatory, NASA.* <http://eoimages.gsfc.nasa.gov/images/imagerecords/439000/39646/bihard_amo_2009213_lrg.jpg>

# Courtship Tanka

## Radhey Shiam

an endless thirst
for the taste of love
sweet or sour matters little
body mind and soul
long to feel warmth of love


sweet whispers behind the curtain
stolen kisses behind the bush
speaking glances on the road
improved relationship
with each courtship step


like wind and ocean
courtship remains ever in motion
builds castle in the air
for the couple
it is paradise on the earth


we work together
sit at one table
I love him
how innocent is he—
he understands not my gesture


I love him
his large innocent eyes
a harmless creature
poor fellow
he responds not


for the first time
I saw in his eyes
longing for me
I have a reason
to smile and dance in glee

when I speak
he turns a deaf ear
when I keep silent
he gets worried
what can I do?


how to tell him
I have a male friend
no lost love
but a friendship
will he believe me?


seeing the boy
I laugh and
throw my purse before him
he picks up the purse
shakes hands with me


my sweet heart,
reading your letter
I feel your breaths
on my cheeks
a feeling of true love

*~India*

# *Painem*

## Alex von Vaupel

My great-grandfather ran a tobacco plantation, in the Dutch East Indies. Belawan Estate was situated in East Sumatra. The local woman who became his concubine, or *nyai*, was my great-grandmother. *Nyai* women lived their lives in the shadows, as servants and second class citizens. Often the same was true for their children, half Indonesian, half Dutch, they didn't belong anywhere.

My great-grandmother's name was Painem. I was always told she was a local woman from North-East Sumatra. Within Sumatra there are many different ethnic groups, each with their own language, customs, and beliefs. Trying to learn about Painem's cultural background, and my Indonesian roots, proved impossible.

There is no record of her origins. The Dutch officials didn't bother to note any additional family names, or her birthplace, that might help to identify her. Based on where they lived, 40 miles South-West from Medan, in the direction of Brastagi, Painem might have been Karo Batak. According to stories told in my family, she was from Aceh, and a princess, but it is unlikely a princess would have ended up a *nyai*. Both the Batak and Aceh cultures have more elaborate naming systems indicating family relationships, rather than just the one name.

Meanwhile any mention of the name Painem I have been able to find, suggests the name is Javanese, in which case it makes more sense that she had only one name, no family name. Was she a Javanese servant who came to work for my great-grandfather? I still have no idea who she really was.

> Painem
> only one name
> and one photo
> to prove
> her existence

> in back of the car
> two dark faces
> a *nyai* with her son
> the white man
> at the wheel

> a name would do
> Dutch officials
> had no interest
> in who she was
> where she came from

> how much truth is there
> to his stories?
> my grandfather
> proud of his mother
> made her a princess

Both the Aceh and Batak people are proud people who fought fiercely against the Dutch, something that was often mentioned in my grandfather's stories. The impression is that his mother, whatever her true origins, was a strong woman. It seems she got her way a little more than other *nyai* did.

The Dutch men did not always recognize their mixed-race children, but my great-grandfather did. He sent them to Holland to live with family and go to school. That is how my grandfather Jan and his older brother and sister came to the Netherlands. Painem could keep her youngest with her a year longer than the other two children.

When Jan was sent to the Netherlands in 1920, Painem accompanied him. They celebrated his seventh birthday on board the SS Oranje. The shipping companies in those days printed their passenger lists in the papers. Only his name appears in the lists. No mention of his Indonesian mother. Painem died in Den Haag a few years later. I'm not sure how she died, I have no record, only a vague memory that someone said it was cold and she was taken ill.

> no mention
> of his Indonesian mother
> in the arrivals list
> Painem
> wasn't newsworthy

> telling stories
> to his grandchild
> he stops short
> of where his mother died
> one cold Dutch winter
> far from home

Idealised, I know, but I always imagine her standing alone, looking out over some beautiful vista, like their family trips to Lake Toba. I want to know who this woman was, who was almost entirely erased from history, except in the memories of her children. You couldn't tell by looking at me, that I am 1/8 Indonesian, but it matters to me that her blood runs through my veins. I wonder how she saw her world, what would she have had to say if she had voice in history?

> a woman
> stands at the edge
> of the crater lake
> water smooth
> under the full moon

> Lake Toba
> shimmers in her eyes
> beneath the quiet surface
> lie battle scars
> of past eruptions

> my heritage
> of guilt and pride
> i'm the great-grandchild of
> a colonist
> and his Indonesian *nyai*

suppressed strands
of DNA —
does it even count
that 1/8 of me
is Indonesian?

> my Dad
> still looks Asian,
> i just tan easily
> and dye my hair
> that shiny black

> finding pride
> in mixed heritage
> laced with guilt
> the task of unlearning
> white privilege

> what stories
> did she have to tell?
> digging deeper
> in search
> of my great-grandmother's garden

*~Indonesia/The Netherlands*

# Sinjo Jan

## Alex von Vaupel

When I was twelve, I asked my grandfather to tell me stories about his youth in Indonesia. The response was an elaborate letter, four pages long, written on a mechanical typewriter. Of course, talking to a child about his own childhood memories, the picture he painted was a pretty one.

My grandfather Jan was half Indonesian, half Dutch, the son of a Dutch colonist and his Indonesian concubine. His father recognized his three children, two sons and a daughter, and sent them to school in the Netherlands.

In his letter he told me all that he could remember about the first six years of his life in Indonesia. He described at length of the workings of his father's tobacco plantation, Belawan Estate: growing and processing the tobacco, the hierarchy of white owners, servants of various levels and ethnic origins. Talking about his past, he rarely mentioned the complex issues of Dutch imperialism, his mixed ethnicity, the position of his mother, her death. The Belawan Estate that emerges from his letter is above all a place full of adventure. All the sights and sounds of the jungle, the animals everywhere. It was a place bustling with activity, with people from many parts of the world bringing their own language and cultures: Batak, Aceh, Javanese, Madurese, Chinese, Japanese, and Dutch.

He enjoyed a lot of freedom in those early years, always outdoors and barefoot. Even as young as five years old he was riding his father's old horse around the plantation, bossing people around because he was the Master's son, though he would get punished for it later. He was known as little master (*tuan kecil*) or young mister (*sinjo* or *sinho*) Jan. That way of life ended just before he turned seven. He was sent to Holland on the steamer *SS Oranje*, accompanied by his mother. He had been very popular with the coolies and the people of the local village, and they threw him a big party or *selamatan* to say goodbye.

all jungle night
the racket of crickets
to be woken
by monkeys shouting
greetings to the sun

earworms*, mosquitos,
*cicaks** and geckoes
snakes, mice and rats:
no keeping the jungle
out of the house

slowly slithering
through the hall
under the bed
nobody bothers the boa
hunting for mice

the water buffalo
too skinny
for milking
canned condensed milk
for the children

Dutch food
6 days out of 7
it would be best for the kids
but always
Indonesian dessert

running around
barefoot
free
except for sundays
when the shoes always hurt

just five years old
riding Dickie
the retired cart-horse
he commanded
the whole plantation

a little fun
in the hard working day
everybody loved
the child master
riding around giving orders

*selamatan*
for the *tuan-kecil* ⸺
*little master*
leaving for school
in cold far Holland

6 years old
his first and last *selamatan*
the night and the people
tasty food
served in palm leaves

travel documents
for young
Sinjo Jan
the thumbprint
on his first passport

a new life
in this strange land
that winter
he saw snow
for the first time

the new brown kid
in the school yard
he already knows:
punch first
introductions later

accustomed
to shoes
being painful
he never asked
for bigger ones

childhood dreams
of a brighter,
warmer sun
his lost world
of emerald green

He remained a free spirit growing up in the Netherlands. He practiced martial arts, and he liked to party. When their father died, my grandfather and his older brother were kicked out by their relatives. At 15 and 18 they had to fend for themselves. Their sister found a man and went to Belgium with him. My grandfather didn't finish school, but he did get diplomas for various office jobs. He joined the army and became a sergeant. During the 5 days of war against the German invasion, 5–10 May 1940, he fought in the Westland. There were not that many Asians in the Netherlands then, so he attracted some attention.

scorched earth tactic
the farm on fire
no place to hide
he jumped into
the slurry pit

rescued from drowning
in dung
they hosed him down
amazed he had brown skin
all over

his stories
about the Second World War
always the funny
never the gore
the destruction

His brother experienced WWII on the other side of the world. He had gone back to Indonesia, and being half Dutch, he ended up in a Japanese internment camp. He survived, but the traumatic experience changed him forever. His sister was apparently deported from her home in Belgium and executed across the border in France. How it happened was never said explicitly. Supposedly the Germans tried to 'force her to marry', and when she and other women refused, they were killed.

non-Aryans
one brother in a Japanese camp
the other fighting the Nazis
their sister captured,
raped, and murdered

Meanwhile, after my great-grandfather returned to the Netherlands, Belawan Estate was taken over by new owners. It was later shut down by the colonial government because the poor living quarters of the coolies had become unacceptable. What was left of Belawan Estate was used by the Japanese as one of their internment camps during WWII. It was a camp for women first and later for men. I didn't know about this until I did a project on the Japanese camps in secondary school and found a reference to Belawan Estate in my books.

ten old barracks
deemed unfit
for coolies to live in
just right
for a prison camp

After the war, my grandfather turned down the offer of a military career and took a desk job, settling into a peaceful family life. Though he was pleased to have a comfortable life with his wife and children, I think he always kept dreaming of a more adventurous life.

he taught me how
to catch a bug
with glass and coaster
after the war
he wouldn't kill a fly

still a soldier
he liked knives
the big guns he never turned in
but his stories
always about peace

sambal
added to every meal
spicing up
the boredom
of Dutch middle class life

what's left now
of that long lost paradise
a yearly visit
to the *Pasar Malam\*\*\**
in Den Haag

*\* 'earworms': in Dutch oorwurm is the same as earworm in English, music that gets stuck in your head. Oorworm is the term for earwigs. In Dutch, and in my grandfather's letter, the two terms are often confused. So he writes about earworms not earwigs. It fits, with all the noisy animals in the house and surrounding jungle.*

*\*\* cicaks are small lizards*

*\*\*\* Pasar Malam: big festive Indonesian market.*

# Indonesian Images of His Youth

## Jade Pandora

a komodo dragon
standing
very still
on the pathway
to our hut

abandoned
on the dock,
the strike and sting
of a jellyfish
to my invading foot

beneath
the walking house
bottle caps,
colorful seashells,
and coral for luck

this morning's catch
smells better
than
the fisherman
who peddles it

tickling my arm
in the dappled light
of the palms,
a pet shrimp
that the sun plays through

ancient stories
unfolding
from ancient fire,
the shadows of puppets
open my mind

*~Indonesia*

lizards
upon lizards
crawling over each other
for the highest place
to worship the sun

riding a boat
to the other island,
my first kiss
runs aground
before landfall

# Morning Raga

### Kath Abela Wilson & *Genie Nakano*

what shall I call you
pink trumpet flower
illusive posing
in a blue sari as you sweep
circles around the tree

> *chakras spin*
> *on a mosaic labyrinth*
> *I follow the color*
> *that vibrates*
> *most under bare feet*

the sound of breathing
in our small room
woken by water birds
visions of cows by the lake
I watch from the upper window

> *down dark stairways*
> *drums and puja bells*
> *racing to catch up*
> *hungry dogs*
> *block a narrow path*

on the ceiling
incense paints
a blossom
stirs the space between
sleeping and waking

> *samadhi smile*
> *turmeric on his third eye*
> *this is for you …*
> *marigold flowers fall*
> *from his hands to mine*

a high ledge
on the landing
a listening place
for swans
by the waterfall

> *tamarind leaves*
> *turn in hot air*
> *I listen for the wind*
> *complete silence*
> *fills the air*

in the small park
an empty tiger cage
door ajar
I shiver without looking back
gaze at yellow hills

> *a door*
> *is left wide open*
> *curtains pulled apart*
> *a moment travels on*
> *sandalwood scented dreams*

~Delhi and Mumbai, India; *Delhi and Jaipor,*
*Rajasthan, India*

# Where is Mount Kinabalu?

## Gerry Jacobson

a campfire flares
in the curtain of night
lighting up
the falling rain—
no one sits there now

The phone rings. A former colleague checking if I'm still alive. Apparently a professor in London wants to talk to me about some work I did on Mount Kinabalu. OMG. Has someone proved me wrong after forty years? I don't really want to know.

But the prof (R. H.) is not trying to prove me wrong. He takes a pioneering geologist for lunch at an olde English pub. Congratulates me on my work. How did I manage in such rugged terrain in those ancient days before GPS? And how did I get involved in this study?

where
is Mount Kinabalu?
it's in old photos
in new emails
it's in my heart . . . my pen

Faded black and white photos of a young Australian geologist with a flowing beard. A golden time, the best of times. We share it, Rae and I, newly married. Assigned to Sabah by the Australian equivalent of Peace Corps. Rae works as a physio at the local hospital. I spend much of my time clambering up and around a great mountain.*

back in time . . .
deep rainforest
rushing streams
slippery boulders . . .
life in front

Mt Kinabalu broods over northern Borneo. I brood too—how soon can I go up it? A mountaineer and here's this dramatic awesome mountain on my doorstep. Rae and I climb it, but we're too eager and go up too fast. I have altitude sickness and she has to support me. After that I make sure I take two days for the ascent from sea level.

A visiting scientific expedition. We climb up the eastern side of the mountain, and out on the unexplored north ridge. Camp on top for a week or so. I map granite structures and also glacial features. The mountain was once capped by ice. Swollen joints from the sojourn at 4000 metres.

Field trips around the mountain. Assisted by a gang of Ibans. They are employed by the Geological Survey and regarded as the best jungle travellers. They carry rice. As we eat the rice I fill up their umbongs with rock specimens. As a tuan I have some small tins of curry to flavour the rice. The protein-hungry Ibans catch rats to supplement their rice. One day I join them in an enjoyable meal of smoke blackened cobra. Is it true that you become what you eat? I think of this every time my yoga teacher gets us to do Bhujangasana, Cobra Pose.

wash in a pool
stand on a boulder
smell of the Earth . . .
all those rainforest
mornings long ago

I navigate and map in the forest by walking up stream channels where the rock is exposed. Air photos show the river courses, and I use a pocket compass to keep track of which section I'm in. Sketch or photograph rock outcrops.

Towards the end of one field trip the Ibans ask me why I keep photographing my geological hammer.

> speckled light
> on leaf litter
> the sound
> of running water
> washes right through me

It's dangerously slippery in the rivers and on waterfalls, and I wear sandshoes. The others are barefoot which is safer but they get more cuts. Leech bites become infected. I lose weight. Emaciated.

Easy friendship with our contemporaries. Young graduates, many from Australian universities. The emerging Malaysian elite. But our corner of paradise turns sour at the end of 1969. Race riots in Kuala Lumpur. No violence in Sabah but things are tense. People imprisoned without trial. We shoulder our packs, pick up our newborn baby and head off.

> wind stirs
> the still deep pool
> reflections waver . . .
> become murky . . .
> I'm thinking again

*~Malaysia*

*\* Author's Note: Mount Kinabalu rises to 4100 m out of equatorial rainforest. It is the highest mountain in Southern Asia between the end of the Himalayan chain and Irian Jaya. It is the dominant feature of the Kinabalu National Park, and is Malaysia's first UNESCO World Heritage Site. Mt Kinabalu is a layered granite intrusion of about 7 million years ago.*

*\*\* The accused Afghan mullah, Mohammad Amin, was arrested and confessed to having sex with the girl after Quran recitation classes at the mosque on May 1.*

*<http://indianexpress.com/article/world/asia/brutally-raped-by-mullah-10-year-old-afghan-girl-faces-murder-by-own-family/>*

# The Mullah and the Green Peach\*\*

## Julie B. Cain

he rips
the flesh of a green peach—
a girl of ten
too young to defend herself
from rape or marriage


easy to hold
to rend a mouthful of tart
juice with the seed—
she's too young to understand
the blame of dishonor


the tree doesn't need
a piece of half-eaten
green fruit—
she asks to return home
not knowing


the sin
of his desire
lies in the peach—
magnanimously
he offers marriage


ripped down
fruit for birds—
too young to choose
between death
or his hunger

*~Afghanistan*

## Patches on the Moon

### Marilyn Humbert

In this place . . .

dark patches
dot the full moon—
spilt ink
spreads . . . staining
my sleep logic

A clinging, syrupy dampness bubbles with sticky prescience knowledge. My skin crawls as I peer through my fingers at dusty shadows dancing in circular patterns. Wind croons from far away. Fog parts and joins, breakers against the shore.

lost in a forest
of stray thoughts—
dreams hide
beneath
a mystic curtain

Like an explorer, a traveller of old, I tread trails scrawled on a map made by the hand of Hercules or Odyssey. I roam lands of myths and elder gods. Puzzle secrets of lost ages.

clouds gather
thunder and lightning—
an acolyte
follows footsteps
of his master

Each day, I stumble from depths of this other place. I wake with mornings' sounds.

grey sky
toss aside your quilt
let the sun shine . . .
I hum, with tiny birds
resting in a dead tree

*~Shangri-La Kunlun Mountains, Nepal*

## Climbing

### Marilyn Humbert

at sea level
voices of snow peaks
sing to me
of wild ancient lands
yeti and yaks

crampons
strapped tight . . .
I follow
the leader
between clouds

wet, cold
red raw hands—
gasping
the thin air
of heaven

balancing
on top of the world
no sound
among snowflakes
but the wind's lullabies

*~Himalaya Mountains Nepal*

## Quiet Dawn

Genie Nakano

it's been a long time
yet I clearly remember
the quietness of dawn
on the Thar desert's
sand dunes of Rajasthan


sound of camel bells
beneath my window . . .
lean forward as my camel
rises from his knees
long pillars in the sand


moonlight shimmers
as we silently carve our way
into a sea of silver sand
my heart beats like a humming bird
i've dreamed this dream before


me and my lover
journeying on the edge of earth
underwater rhythms
of an ancient time
when we followed stars


speak no words
listen only to the wind
leave behind
no footprints in the sand
we create eternity


the spell is broken
just beyond a campfire burns
warm chai and family
greet us, with the dawn
the sun's about to rise

*~India*

## Winter Song Bird

Genie Nakano

hot, hotter, hottest
the three seasons of Thailand
sweat pours down
between my breasts
it's Winter in Thailand


she speaks Thai to me,
flattered, I pretend understanding
this Thai woman so beautiful
shyly I tell her . . .
I'm Japanese American


*sawadikup, sawadikup*
my hands pressed together
held close to my heart
as we bow to each other
I want to stay forever


Buddha sat here,
Shiva danced on these temple grounds
the king of Thailand wears pink
monks float in saffron robes
the rainbows starts and ends here


night market
a thousand woks on fire
essence and sizzling sounds
each bite takes us higher to
a gastronomic heaven


I let the caged bird
fly free . . . .
knowing full well
a thousand more
will be captured

*~Thailand*

## The Gatekeeper at Yazd

### Kath Abela Wilson

We came through the narrow entrance to the Towers of Silence greeted by his nod. The low dirt hills were flat-topped mounds rising stark against the dull sky. A few visitors wandered around. I overheard that the families had just left and the corpse was finished by the birds. We saw nothing of this, but the air felt stirred by scavengers. It was hard to breathe, but there was no scent. At the gate we hesitated. His turban bound dignity and handsome figure did not give away his age.

at the last minute
he gave us
a knowing look
gestured at my camera
and posed

~Towers of Silence, Zoroastrian burial grounds, Yazd, Iran

## Monkey Business

### Kath Abela Wilson

The road to Agra was dense with cars, cows, trucks, buses, auto rickshaws, horse and buggies, man-drawn wagons, small vans for four, packed with twenty, back to back. Speed was optional, horns mandatory, there were no lanes. At least we had a good driver. He fit his five foot cab into every two foot space at about 70 mph. It all came to a standstill as we approached our destination. A light tapping on our back window.

monkey
with a stick
a man pushes forward
the small metal cup in his hand
reads Taj Mahal

~Iran

# Adoption

## *Tanka from Nepal*

## Michael G. Smith

orphanage birth day—
a *didi* places swaddled
sixteen-month Suntali
in Trish-mom's eager arms
clouds happily crying too

*~Bal Mandir Orphanage, Kathmandu*


we stop at a shop
for Suntali's visa pic
the Dalai Lama hugs
a monk and blesses mother
and daughter in my photo too

*~Kathmandu*


she is peace
and contentment    we know
she knows who mom is
what the Cheerio box holds
my book-light's close-open magic

*~Kathmandu*


after arriving
at the Galaxy Hotel
we are served hot chai
and ginger snaps in the chill air
bored soldiers marching below

*~Chisapini Hill*


a bamboo swing swings
sleeping she on my lap through
this boisterous city's
island of still air    daisies
lazing in a copper bowl

*~The Garden of Dreams, Kathmandu*


mom spins prayer wheels
and lights butter lamps
for her daughter
old Buddha smiles   holy
monkeys scamper and play

*~Swayambhunath, The Monkey Temple, Kathmandu*


she slurps milky froth
for my dark coffee
turns a magazine's
colored pages   the world open
full of butterflies, sweet tastes

*~Hotel Yak and Yeti, Kathmandu*


on green grass
she takes her first steps
her tiny fingers
holding my much larger ones
her red sneakers chiming in

*~Kathmandu*

# Pilgrimage

## *Tanka from India*

## Michael G. Smith

Japanese pilgrims
Chinese too awakening
their enlightenment
sit beneath the sacred fig—
one tree many branches

*~Mahabodhi Temple, Bodh Gaya*

on the guesthouse roof
a monkey and her child
steal my journal and pen
hiss when i lift a broom
their taste bitter, they drop them

*~Varanasi*

beneath a full moon
the boatman quietly treads
his oars    funeral pyres
illuming the ghat, the priest
asks us to help the sick, the old

*~River Ganga, Varanasi*

on stage Lord Shiva
villagers farmers tradesmen
monks mothers merchants
sing We Shall Overcome—
gospel school in the far east

*~Tibetans Children's Village School, Upper Dharamsala*

four Tibetans carry
a fifth's immolated corpse
compatriots follow
chant ring bells    power failure!
candles light the blackened street

*~McLeod Ganj*

roadside tire stall
a man dressed in a pink dhoti
and flip-flops pounds a tire
with an awl and mallet
rice fields meet the horizon

*~National Highway 2 between Varanasi and Gaya*

in the waters
Nancy washes stone Buddhas
two boys bathe    splish splash!
a cow enjoys my scratching
the soft space behind her ears

*~River Ganga, Rishikesh*

Shoe Doctor Ramesh
asks if my sandals need cleaning
after I circumambulate
the Kora    his sign saying
all is possible in India

*~McLeod Ganj*

filthy and shoeless
two toddlers walk the main street
morning up
evening down
I see them all day now

*~Mussoorie*

# An Imaginary Tour with the Buddha

## Richard St. Clair

The Mayadevi Temple
in Lumbini seems to glow
marking the place
where Maya gave birth to you
O World Turner!


Here in Kapilavastu
as a youth you saved a bird
whom Devadatta wounded
with an arrow -
and you have saved me too!


O Master,
Show me where you sat
in deep meditation
beneath the pipal tree
until you achieved release!


Mahabodhi Temple
at Bodhgaya
reaches upward to the sky
it lifts my heart -
so much more your teaching, Master!


The Deer Park at Sarnath!
Where you first turned
the Wheel of the Dharma -
and in my mind
I stand upon that spot!


Jetavana!
Here you preached
eight hundred sutras,
Lord Buddha!
May I remember just one!


Tell me of the miracle
on this sacred spot of Rajgir
where you once subdued
the charging elephant
sent by evil Devadatta!


The Pillar of Asoka
two thousand years old
reminds this visitor
that this is where you
once walked, once talked


In my mind I see myself
atop sacred Vulture Peak
breathing the same air
you yourself breathed
those thousands of years ago


A dozen monks
in bright saffron robes
atop the mountain
remembering the words
that you once preached


On this sacred ground,
tell me Lord Buddha
where are the 84,000
in whom you raised Bodhi mind
here at Vaisali?


Today the rains
pour down in torrents
like that day
when you converted
the multitudes

The ancient frieze
of the monkey offering you
an alms bowl
filled with honey
fills my heart with joy!


On this sacred ground
of Kusinagara
you breathed your last
entering into the same nirvana
where I will follow, Master!

*~United States*

## *Night in Yazd*

## Kath Abela Wilson

sometimes the breast of a woman
curves over the sleeping city
wakeful babies
we travel the milky way
into her dream


sometimes
under the thin plucked eyebrow
of moon the tear
of a woman
shows the directions

in the night we know
the woman is naked
we know by the falling
sparkles of her necklace
she had no time to take off


we know
the woman smiles
her smile grows larger
until it covers
her face


at night
when you kneel
on your bed
over her and think
that you have her


perhaps you call her
name
in love
or even in anger
she has already disappeared


she
has slipped
into your body
in the night
with her tidings


she
moves you
she moves
your brush your pen
at her whim

*~Yazd, Iran*

## Elephant Island

### Kath Abela Wilson

trying to cross
a Delhi street
I bobble my head
the best I can do
without wings


home from India
with my eyes closed
a mouse
who swallowed
an elephant


as if my body
was made for this
tamboura
in India I learned by heart
a different scale


*~Delhi, Mumbai, and Elephant Island, off the coast
of Mumbai, India*

## Powder

### Rebecca Drouilhet

No one knows how or why the young mother
became addicted. We never thought heroin could
find its way into our little neighborhood. After
her death, we planted flowers in her memory.


a killing frost
glitters on moonflowers . . .
an orphan
reaches out to touch
the passing blossoms


*~Picayune, Mississippi, USA*

## For My (Lost Not Beat) Generation

### Chen-ou Liu

During his two-year mandatory military service, my graduate school classmate, who hand-copied *On the Road* in his freshman year, constantly forgot to say "Yes, Sir" and "No, Sir," chain-smoked on duty, and was found once reading a holey edition of *Playboy* when he should have been drilling. After completing the service, he came back to his hometown, found a 9-to-5 job, became a company man, got married and had two kids, later moved to a bedroom community of Taipei, the capital city of Taiwan (formerly known as the Republic of China), and fully embraced the emerging IKEA culture, keeping up with the Joneses.

first winter light
on the empty side
of the bed
my friend phones me, rambling
about *The Dharma Bums*

at twilight
I murmur to myself
"I should have . . . "
echoing and echoing
after he ended the call

*~Taiwan*

## Perspective

### Joann Grisetti

In season, I can buy a *mikan* for about five yen—less than two cents. They are juicy and segmented like a tangerine, but with a different, slightly tart flavor. Fruits with thick skins that are peeled and discarded are perfectly safe for us to eat fresh, and I do enjoy them on a hot sticky summer day. Often street vendors come right by our house with large baskets of *mikan*. *Mikan* soda we buy at a little street market near our house, and return the bottles to be reused. Each bottle of *mikan* soda comes with a small glass marble at the bottom and holds about six to eight ounces of cooled juicy drink.

sweetly tart
juicy lips swallow—
the marble shifts
my view of the world
a new perspective

*~Sasebo Japan*

# my Japanese home town: a tanka string

## Sanford Goldstein

thought Shibata
was a quiet, non-violent
place,
in today's newspaper
three dead women in a field

trying to get
to my tanka café,
find the roads blocked,
a three-day holiday in the town
for those who want to fight

how thankful
am I for my tanka café called
"The Second Movement"—
for ten years the same supper
and the spilling of fifteen tanka

the coffee Master
of my tanka café a violinist,
his wife a pianist,
often special concerts held
in that crowded space

as shop doors
close once it gets dark out,
another world appears,
how colorful the brush drawings
when their shutters are down

a surprise
to learn of a yearly festival
for Sakae Osugi,
the anarchist killed in 1923,
ten of his childhood years in Shibata

how often
we drive to various restaurants
in Shibata,
one Chinese, one a cafeteria,
one open twenty-four hours for workers

~Shibata, Japan

# Epithalamium

## Natsuko Wilson

*Cape Cod, Massachusetts, June 22, 2014*

Sitting at the Bay
One bright day in June
I sing
The tune of "Greensleeves"
Out loud to the ocean

A little sea gull
Is waddling, and stops
To sit beside me—
We both watch Oscar swimming
Far in the ocean

A gentle breeze
Reminds me of the moment that
Sabrina's black hair
waving in the wind, and
sending more blue to the sky

Finding a love
Her eyes suddenly brightened up
Three summers ago
Now I see the ocean smiling and celebrating,
Under the silver light

Opening my eyes
I watch the white clouds
moving slowly in the sky
As if a family of whales is taking a trip
To the South

Then, quietly
Oscar's hand is
On my shoulder
Freezingly shocked
I give him the towel

"How was the water?"
I asked
"Wonderful"
Was the answer, totally bored with us
A little sea gull is flying away

*~Cape Cod, Massachusetts, USA*

# From New York to Toronto

## Rodney Williams

*For Meg*

skate-boards rattle
down this East Village street
at 3.00 a.m.—
waiting all our lives to sing
the city that never sleeps


National Museum
of the American Indian
on Bowling Green—
chiselled into stone below:
U. S. Bankruptcy Court


patisserie walls
with movie star autographs . . .
workers in fluoro
quaffing racks of short-blacks
thump their chests: We can do it!


Canada geese
by the Statue of Liberty—
Ellis Island
Migration Museum
closed by Hurricane Sandy


Ground Zero—
his wife at his elbow
a New York fireman
makes a charcoal rubbing
of a workmate's name


heading north
towards our son long gone . . .
on a plate of rock
in the middle of the Hudson
a house three stories high


in plain view
behind a pampas grass field
two roe deer
believing they're hidden . . .
oh babe keep watching my back


on an updraft
above the hydro plant
vultures glide—
in an upstate county
election day bunting


as wheels on rails
click with her prayer beads
one passenger
chants in Chinese . . .
Niagara Falls the border


below
a woodpeckers' hole
carved in bark
a Cupid's heart
that could have been ours

*~United States*

# Hannah Paul

The sky
Hues of tangerine
Scattered souls
Of blood oranges
Bleeding in my mouth


I have no need
To be frivolous
Each breath
I breathe
Is accounted for


*One more to go*
She said
Lighting her
Fortieth cigarette
Of the day


The moon
A waning gibbous
Tonight
More beautiful
Than full


A pack
Of cigarettes
Her ashen face
She remembers
why She quit smoking


They fly
Fluttering in rhythm
To unbridled passions
Pecking surreal kisses
I saw sparrows make love

Confide in my fallow heart
Unfurl your secrets
Rest your burden
On me—
I want to crush your Spirit


The highs & lows
Of the
*Anser indicus*
Are no match
To the junkies


Proliferated insanity
Voluntary darkness
My sane insanity
Why must I conform
To your norm


Sleep
A stew delis'
Everyone eats of it
But when I do
It's undercooked

*~Pakistan*

# Nilufer Y. Mistry

our road,
an avenue of trees . . .
her blossoms,
let loose, over-run
this summer-sky

us. siblings. smiling
from an old photograph
crammed together
on an old studio bench
bright-eyed . . . peas-in-a-pod

scrambling
among grey-clouds
a deepening glow . . .
as summer-rain writes
the rhythm of sunlight

smoke . . .
this lingering taste of war.
sour blood
& mangled metal
all-over my tongue

crying . . .
pushed out from a womb of war,
hatred births
from the stony confines of Gaza,
spilling her blood, into all our homes

running through
his sprawl of written-words,
this  s p i n e  of thought;
holding,
each branching rib of verse

our old chimney
smokeless through summer
flares-up
with fledgling-flutters
. . . warbles with bird-song

on tip-toes
snub-nose in the air
she holds a breath . . .
—five-year-old, trying to be
as  t a l l  as her evening-shadow

feeding on filtered-light,
chirping
through shifting-shadows
of summer-leaves,
the flicker of house sparrows

lit . . .
by a sudden shaft of sunlight,
the empty river road
flooded
in amber

old-growth forest
undisturbed . . . dripping rain . . .
the wisdom of her history
hidden
in her thousand growth-rings

trying
to decipher your silence
i wade
through a marsh of darkness
still lost . . . unable to reach you

the sound
of sunlight
as it  b~r~e~a~k~s
on running water
—glistening river-stones

hovering at dusk
along the wooded-trail
like an apparition . . .
a ghost of gnats
spiralling, in the summer-heat

the smoothness
of a simple verse . . .
how it
s l i d e s  into being
. . . like a summer-sky


full-moon
round, like Brie
. . . full-fat
drunk, hanging-low
drowning in a Merlot-night


skimming the surface of streams
spawning
amongst loose stones & shallow crevices
breathless . . . salmon swim up
open-mouthed river-estuaries


transparent . . .
the lightness
of summer
woven amongst
the hush of river-reeds


like a forest-fern
first-light
unfurls her fronds
into
the new-day


breath of their eyes
their child
now gone forever
lost . . .
among the  f o l d  of stars

laughing,
buttercups
tumble down the slope
   c r a w l    u  n
garden-fencing     d
                e
       r


silence
walks with us
down the gravel path
to the twilit river
   . . . you can hear her footsteps


a summer breeze . . .
trees whisper their dreams
a thousand leaves
fluttering
like prayer-flags


here, where blue sky
floats along slow water
& dragonflies hover
among the rush of whispering reeds
—the smile of our summer-river


the fading gloam
just a strand of light
echoing . . .
quivering, like the last note
of a violin


they flood into the auditorium
like pilgrims, flocking to a shrine
to hear
an old poet, speak  . . .
his Book of Longing*

   *Book of Longing by Leonard Cohen


sullied  . . . her fall from grace
from an ancient heaven
built on dogma;
b a r r e d  a re-entry to life
—falling-star


empty . . .
I dive into the shadow
of his written-word
searching for the sand-vein . . .
for that spine of meaning

bobby-pinned, pig-tailed
squinting through a playground-sun
this bridge of brown freckles!
spanned across
her five-year-old smile


a lone star
on the rim of twilight
roots, into the moist darkness
birthing a million stars . . .
like butterflies


like mermaids
singing to the moon
the c r y of hump-back whales
their bodies lit
in ocean-phosphorescence


curled up
tender
like tiny foetuses,
fiddleheads dream
among the woodland fern


our lives
built together,
a shared history . . .
a time-line
of gathered stones


we pass each other
seeing but silent.
like tall-ships on a painted ocean
sailing in different directions
yet witnessing . . . the same sunrise


our lives emerge
through the darkness
of a million light-years
in these twists of breath & light
—shimmering strands of cosmos


unmoored
he drifts away from life's purpose
still searching
for that lost compass
. . . his connection to the stars


his breath,
a part of this sunrise.
i look along the empty shore
catch a glimpse, as he dives,
a silver arc . . . returning into ocean


heading home
through heavy rain
car headlights
s e a r the empty darkness
branding the night


in his hovel
cradling his sleeping child
he looks up at a skyful of stars
dreaming-up happiness
sweeping want & hunger into a dark corner


dawn's desire
swims naked
wanton
in a flawless
river of sky


caught between sun & shadow
trailing nebulous fins
& flickering tails
the koi-pond dances . . .
dabbling . . . diaphanous in light


first light-fall …
a silent field
filled with wild-flowers
still asleep
breathing darkness . . . breathing light

morning
walks-into the l i f t
of a hundred sunlit wings …
white feathers float down, silent . . .
to the empty, cobbled square


like a fine strung-string
of a violin
twilight reverberates . . .
fusing the light & hum
of evening hours, with night


autumnal weather . . .
she hovers over that fine-line . . .
an open blue sky
could change to a brooding storm
on a whim & flick of her hair


their children
'home'
for the summer-break;
their house
h u m s  again


slow summer-river
her cellophane ripples
silently wrapping
storing . . .
this blue summer-sky

y e t  another sunset
dissolving into
y e t  another night
of  w a r
over Gaza


a dream of peace.
where the laughter
of  a l l  our children, rings.
pealing, like a morning angelus
rising into an albescent-sky


hot august.
a hint of Autumn
among the maples.
Summer, still gives her
. . . the cold-shoulder


hot August
burns the backyard-grass
still,
a hint of Autumn rust
spreads among the maples


sky,
fills
with morning.
this ocean
. . . flooded in l i g h t


anchored boats bob . . .
a line along
the creaking wooden pier.
metal-rigging jostling, clanging,
. . . like rusted wind-chimes


sparrows return to the old tree
tiny, little leaf-like shadows . . .
they flicker . . .
a fluttering filigree
of evening-light & shadow

our open
kitchen-window;
so many sunlit-songs
from unseen summer birds
frame this blue morning


sun-burnt laughter
as children swim in streams
smelling of summer;
sunshine tangled in wet hair
waving . . . like sea-anemones

wordlessly,
the moon
& sky
i n h a l e ...
this shared summer-night


my sunny
summer garden;
the flickering
black shadows
of white butterflies


another dawn.
an egg-shell sky cracks-open,
letting,
another new day seep-in . . .
y o l k  & all


on grubby knees
surrounded by light
& her summer-roses;
under her straw-brim
. . . her sun-speckled smile


the light
along with
the blue-morning,
lies tangled around,
our spinning sun-catcher


light,
spun through
our sun-catcher;
now this  b l u e
summer-day


the slow drift,
of summer-days
spinning light . . .
yet this
b e n d i n g  into autumn


against a quiet
afternoon sky
Mount Baker
dormant . . . dreaming
among the clouds


rumbling,
our grey-sky
rain-stitched . . .
to the
swollen ocean


new morning.
soft . . . velveteen . . .
arching her back
she walks on soft-paws
p u r r s  into light


hovering over
long mountains,
twilit . . .
lightning sparks
a september-storm


lightning flares
over twilit mountains.
wind-whipped, thunderclouds roll . . .
bits of Autumn wedged
in September's gloam


before sunrise
the empty prayer-hall
still full of shadows, stirs awake;
the brass Buddha's smile
caught, in the dying lamp-light


blue heron
solitary 'fisherman'
wading along a shallow shoreline;
wind-ruffled belly-feathers
up-lit, by water-reflections

# Kala Ramesh

new day
b l o o m s . . .
unfolding
velvet petals
—like a summer-rose


rambling rose . . .
their mad summer-scramble
exploring the season
trampling
light


cool rain . . .
how the colours
of the steaming desert
deepen . . .
horizon to horizon


rust of a dry desert-river
deep scar through gorges
& red canyons
a convoluted, atrophied umbilical
that once joined earth to ocean


morning clouds
. . . a d r I f t . . .
like dreams.
our hopes,
have a silver-lining


sun, pouring through,
sky, floating on water;
blue heron
wades through
morning reflections


wet kayak glistens;
floating, it l i s t e n s
to the silver lake,
—polka-dotted
by autumn-rain

*~Canada / India*


potatoes
can't be boiled twice
he always says . . .
holding back the urge to ask
I leave things unexplained


one red kite
holds the world at bay
and life
on one held breath
ignites a womb


days go by
when nothing moves
as I wish . . .
            the crows
extra chatty today


today I am
a sucked-out orange . . .
time vanishes
into the computer
as words swarm


his abuses
heaped on every driver
on the road . . .
a lullaby
for our little son

*~India*

# Asni Amin

Afghan sky
the light of the crescent moon
shrouded in fog . . .
beneath sky blue burkas
eyes that can no longer cry


night journey
Masjidil Haram
to Masjidil Aqsa . . .
a thousand veils
lifted at dawn


hajj pilgrimage
I leave everything
to come to You . . .
one day I will really leave
all behind


Syrian refugee camp
he listens for the sound
of day breaking . . .
the things I take
for granted


Arab spring
one by one petals fell
into the Nile . . .
dreams of the pharoah
crumbling to dust

*~Singapore*

# Hema Ravi

daughter's school work
she traces her fingers
on the writing—
reality hits her hard
nothing left to pay the fee

*~Chennai, India*

# Ana Prundaru

under the clouds of sorrow
passing fading rose petals
we row back tonight
the ceaseless depth of our love
settles down the waves at sea

*~India*

# Samantha Sirimanne Hyde

rustling bo* leaves
hint of burning palm oil
. . . walking alone
among gum trees
I dream of my other life

*~Grabben Gullen, NSW, Australia*

*bo: Ficus religiosa or sacred fig*


adam's peak*
floating above clouds
I trudge too slow . . .
missing the sunrise
forgetting my prayers

*~Central Highlands, Sri Lanka*

*Adam's Peak: a sacred mountain in Sri Lanka*


hurrying
from the train station
into a drizzle
a boy races past me, yelling
. . . *go home curry muncher*

*~Denistone, NSW, Australia*


back again
in the tropical heat
I grumble . . .
an outsider here
an outsider there

*~Colombo, Sri Lanka*


subtle, yet clear
that shift in her voice
hearing my accent
outside in the mall
pigeons are shooed off

*~Sydney, NSW, Australia*


migrating away
without making amends
now too late
this lesson in hubris
as I read your obituary

*~Denistone, NSW, Australia*


meditating at dawn . . .
unwelcome thoughts
intrude endlessly
raindrops seep through
an ill-thatched roof

*~Blackheath Meditation Centre, NSW, Australia*


leaving work
my bus soared sky-high
from a bomb
over forty lives gone . . .
in that dazing way of karma

*~Colombo, Sri Lanka, 1987*


you and I, a bad link
crisscrossing long paths
across samsara…
gum leaves tossed about
in stormy wintry winds

*~Colombo, Sri Lanka*


makes me smile
this handmade crochet
made as a child
at my grandma's side
a skill now forgotten

*~Colombo, Sri Lanka*

# Ernesto P. Santiago

carrier pigeons
racing back and forth—
against instinct
I follow
my own path, God's will


crescent moon rises,
offering a sense of warmth
—your curves & edges,
I put them into words:
two cultures, one love


with clear skies
sailing between tides
a leaf boat—
my first child wishes
his father's home


no work, no pay:
she grooms her flesh
into the system
of the flesh—
what worms would not want?


beach walk—
I create footprints
where waves are
drawn into
my inner sanctum


dragons & dungeons—
a child, a child, a child
through another war,
out of wars into a war,
this "me" I never had

these fruit bats—
crossing borders,
I rest my ass
between the never
and the night

*~Philippines*

# Sonam Chhoki

black hibiscus heads
toll the ancient votive bells
of Paro Tak-sang . . . *
I wake to monodic sounds
of a critical care unit

*\* Paro Tak-sang: "Tiger's Nest" in the north-western valley of Paro is one of the oldest and most sacred shrines in Bhutan. Its origins date back to the 8th century when the Tibetan Buddhist saint, Guru Rimpoche arrived in Bhutan from Tibet. Legend has it that he flew on the back of a tiger and established the shrine. A fire broke out in the main temple in 1998. Although the sacred relics were rescued and saved many Bhutanese felt this to be a portentous tragedy for the nation. It was rebuilt and restored by 2005.*


half-awake
listening to birds at sunrise
I ask: what would death be like:
a rapid loss of grasp
or a slow unclasping


about to be swatted
a fly hums like the drone
of chanting monks . . .
does it have some memory
of a karmic link with me?

the Kabuki
actor in woman's guise
dies to save *her* lover
we wipe furtive tears
at this tableaux of sacrifice


an early photo
of father in spectacles
I never saw him wear . . .
it seems he too once made
sartorial statements


back home
from a fortnight in Paris
everything is overgrown
I play my new CD:
'*Non, je ne regrette rien*'


to be the eldest!—
undivided parent's love
for the first few years
and later the privilege
to light their pyres*

> *\* Open-air cremation is the funerary practice in Bhutan. The eldest offspring (male or female) performs the main ritual role in the funerary rites for the parents.*


black shadows
of weeping cypress spread
over the dzong ruins  . . . *
this premonitory silence
of our sacred past

> *\* Drukgyel Dzong is a fortress-monastery built in 1649 by Shabdrung Ngawang Namgyel, the founder of the Bhutanese theocratic state to commemorate his victory over the invading Tibetan army. It was destroyed in a fire in 1951 and now lies in ruins in the upper part of the north-western valley of Paro overlooking the old trade route to Tibet.*


waking from
a dream of routes not taken
in the scrim of dawn
the Thimphu Chu* glitters
like shattered glass

> *\* Thimphu: capital of Bhutan; Chu: river in Dzongkha, the lingua franca of Bhutan.*


fog-bound valley—
the full-throated honk
of a Great Hornbill
beckons me to the veranda
from the deep hold of dreams

> *The Great Hornbill is found in the evergreen forests of the lower valleys of Bhutan. This particular incident is based in the perpetually fog-covered valley of Gedu, south-western Bhutan.*

## John Tehan

you visit on the DL
with your taboo desires
as dark as your *lund* . . .*
later, sated, you return home
respectable again

~*Upper East Side / Manhattan, New York City*

> *\*lund: Hindi slang for penis*

# Payal A. Agarwal

mid-afternoon
soaked to skin
from scorching sun
i stand with strangers atop rickety bus
for a glimpse of Mughal monument—Taj Mahal

in velvety darkness
with the moon winking
i immerse Ganesha idol
in the waves of sea
with tears pouring down my face

dusk
home lighted with colorful diyas,
prayers offered to Goddess Lakshmi—
i burst crackers with my new family
a month after my marriage

late summer evening
stuck in a traffic jam
i listen to old hindi songs
that sounds like
the bleating of calfs

day after day
cooking South Indian food
on a dusty roadside stall
i fill strangers' bellies
come rain or sunshine

reclining Buddha
without delay fulfill
my wish of a child
even before i leave
the temple premises

*~India*

# Ram Krishna Singh

With mordant comments
he tries to geld a standpat
in a feminists' meet
and turns a sook
at tea break

My thinning hairs
wave in the bath tub
clog the drain
with soap bubbles deride
my baldness

Visits unannounced
the bodiless god of love—
sweeping the earth and
decking the street with kolam
one more bride, one more wedding

Seeking shelter
under the golden wings
of Angel Michael
a prayer away now
whispers the moon in cloud

He doesn't drink water
for the disgusting things
fish do in it
but enjoys fishing and frying
the catch at the river side

*~Dhanbad, India*

# Pravat Kumar Padhy

the Ganges flows
with the thin moon
godly-chant
from far off distance
resonates for the departed soul

harvest moon
over the golden field
the old man
murmurs to the breeze
holding his trembling lips

remote village
in the dense hill side
the native language
they speak is full of melody
rumbling with the braided stream

villagers look up
at the distant pale sky
a lone frog
in the narrow lane leaps
with footprints of hope

gentle rustling
of the tender leaves
the grandmother
caresses the newborn humming
the melodious desert folk song

sunlit morning
over youthful blossoms
Mother Teresa
with sacred gift of love
rekindles the garden of hope

speechless display
of musical instruments
I recount
peeping into the past
resonance of antique world

tender breeze
whispers something
in deep midnight
the new moon brightens
the tone of my loneliness

morning sun
over the tribal hut . . .
sublime smile
of her daughter reposes
promises of enduring warmth

in deep silence
tender breeze whispers
to the new moon
brightens the tone of
twilight and my loneliness

blinks of red light
flash back my memories
silently I recount
guiding my little daughter
crossing the zebra square

waves after waves
closely follow together
returning home
the grand family enjoys
the forgotten smiles

fragrance of love
carefully the flower preserves
in foggy morning
she gently nurses the wounds
of deep misunderstanding

gentle rustling
of the tender leaves
the grandmother
caresses the newborn
humming song of the nightingale

~India

# Radhey Shiam

television is
dustbin of the society
dirty people
find pleasure
in fouls and filth


a naked lady dances
before the statue of Goddess Kali
devotees dance around her
thinking her to be
real Goddess Kali


a hermit rests
under a Peepal tree
a donkey comes
and takes rest
before the hermit


full moon
a fairy dances on the lawn
a man rushes to hug her
she kicks down the man
and flies away


the tree stands
under which we met
decades ago
still I breathe in
your fragrance of love


so called holy person
lives on donations
unearned wealth
which defiles their
bodies minds and souls

before election
*you are my father*
*please vote for me*
after election
*who are you*


preaching
words of scriptures
to blockheads
is like
casting pearls before swine


a lovely lady enjoys moon light
sitting on the roof
her neighbour comes
and rapes her
she could not cry for help


a beggar spoke to the king
*I am the real king*
*I can move any where*
*without security*
*but you can not*


holding a balloon I flew
to Lahore then to Kabul
Moscow, Berlin, France
and at last landed
at Buckingham Palace

*~India*

# Aruna Rao

dipping
on the shoreline
the red sun
can you not take it
and fill the parting of my hair?

*~Puri, Orissa, India*


the summer sun
throws itself on the salt desert
shimmering like ice—
when did Antarctica
join the west coast of India?

*~Kutch, Gujarat, India*


my lap-top
is a parasite on the inverter
behold the load shedding:
the tubelight that was so bright
suddenly now flickers


evening jog
the taste of ghee and spices
change every corner
turning around, I remember
mother's old recipe

*~NOIDA, Uttar Pradesh, India*


in your smell
I hear the October moon
growing louder
so does the henna's colour
and my pounding heart

for twenty years
you carried this lantern
until I took it
I had never imagined
my shadow would fall on you


my pounding heart
in tandem with your excitement
such wide eyes
the Gods must wonder
how the Yamuna flooded with fear


treasure hunting
in the Yamuna river
for your love
all I find is fear
mixed with plastic

*~New Delhi, India*


this tug-of-war
between the sun and the moon
is it for eternity?
it scares me, that the moon
is always there, in your shadows


I know not
whether it is the sun or moon
that keeps me awake
but the merry-go-round's horse
is the one on the ferris wheel

*~near Surajkund, Haryana, India*

# Anupam Sharma

commuters
wait for the rain to stop
under the tin roof . . .
the smell of brewing tea
makes the strangers talk


the sun
plays hide and seek with clouds
on a monsoon day—
his desperate eyes look up
and then at the dry farm


a moonless night . . .
earthen candles dispel
the darkness
to cast flickering shadows
inside an isolated hut


holy threads
tied around the triveni tree . . . (1)
unsaid wishes
seeking prosperity
through all the seasons


at the sweets' shop
he sees the worker making
round jalebis . . . (2)
the boiling oil fries it
while he thinks about his life


ashes
and flowers silently float
on the river . . .
ephemeral life surrenders
to traverse a new path


dusty colors
fill the air on Holi . . . (3)
masks
of identity dissolve
as hearts forgive the past


women sing
folk songs on the sangeet night . . . (4)
the bride
lost in her thoughts
dreams of harmonic future


temple bells
echo amid the walls . . .
the voice
of conscience becomes
louder and speaks the truth


her wrinkled hands
shiver as she touches
grandson's head . . .
pure blessings release
as she gives a faint smile

*~India*


*1) triveni: a tree considered very holy in India*

*2) jalebi: a sweet dish which is somewhat circular and twisted in shape*

*3) Holi: one of the major festivals in India, when people play with powdered colors*

*4) Sangeet: an auspicious ceremony held in the Hindu marriages*

# Pavithra Satheeshkumar

Monsoon

After a torrid
love affair in the summer,
grey clouds pour down on
naked western ghats starting
a soaking consummation.


Yugadi

Mango leaf festoons,
oil-bathed kids wearing new clothes,
neem and jaggery,
equinox Sun and full Moon
swing us into the new year.


For Heaven's Sake

No green in the skies
except for the northern lights.
Knowing Shakespeare's
green eyed monsters, nature hasn't
put jealousy in her stars!


Perversion

A saké drinking lewd
poet had two mischievous
kids out of wedlock.
The younger Haiku was three
and the older Tanka five.

~Waco, Texas, USA

# Janet Qually

strumming songs
on an esraj folk instrument
at the end of a pier
my feet dangle
in the timeless current

~Sri Lanka


jungle vines
lace through the trees
along a bowered trail
I glimpse a feral child
who will believe me?

~Cambodia


Arabian Sea
the cooperative wind
billows our sails
a refreshing escape
from daily crowds

~Pakistan


water buffalo
work the paddy field
a strong team
do we pull together
as well as them?

~Bangladesh


skilled handlers
guide their elephants
to the riverbank
loud trumpets
and blown water

~India

# Autumn Noelle Hall

what Karma?
for the child dropping ants
in the spiderweb
hunger looms larger
than death

*~India*

asking to borrow
the earrings I dangle
from her crown
White Tara at royal ease
on my night table

*~Nepal*

sleeping beneath
a brass bodhi tree
the mudra
of he who sculpted it
shaping my dreams

*~Nepal*

meditation
the antique thangka draws me
into the cave
of the blind visionary
and his sherpa merchant

*~Tibet*

two gold cups
placed before Kuanyin
one half full
one half empty
of compassion

*~China*

Namaste
bowing to the Divine
in the heron
in the pond, why do I turn
my eyes from my reflection?

*~India*

Shiva Nataraja
I have only two hands
to hold this fire
can I create without
destroying myself?

*~India*

sometimes
when no one else is looking
Ganesh and I
have a mad dance and laugh
at our jiggling bellies

*~India*

# Barbara A. Taylor

*Some snippets of my travel to India, way back:*


so surreal—
pushing a washing machine
on the dusty road
a wizened man trails
ambling elephants


two hours notice
if I wanted showers
. . . above my head
bright eyes of little boys
pouring hot water


at the stone well
a swagger of colour
in swaying hips . . .
when turning the tap
I remember her


on the wrong side
noisy garish trucks
dodge between
the colourful crowd
and the cow

*~India*

# Grunge

too depressed
to write
but happy for
the self
contradiction


my cat likes
rice, beansprouts,
bread, pizza,
and the still beating
hearts of rodents


unrepentant
I watch
the eagle
as it snaps
up my liver


memorial day
and he remembers
his legs
left on the
battlefield


having reached 28
already i've lived
twice as long as
the 14 year old
with the razor predicted

*~United States*

# Mariko Kitakubo

silent
deep black
soil—
dead jungle
were gods here?

*~Northern part of Vietnam by Cyclo*


Milky Way
like a sleeping buddha
on the Mekong—
history is settling
in bottom of the river

*~by the Mekong, in Vietnam*


Ha Long Bay
is the mother of fog
harboring
the old silver scales
of dragons

*~during the cruise of Ha Long Bay in Vietnam; Ha
"Long" means "dragon".*


searching for the gods
ousted from deep forests—
karst mountain
suddenly out
of the misty sea

*~at the edge of the Ha Long Bay, Vietnam*


in the distance
a heap of
jack fruits
look like skulls—
dust on the horizon

*~at the twilight: in rural North Vietnam*

# Rebecca Drouilhet

golden leaves
twirl into winter
a coin
for the ferryman
in this world of passages


crossing the bridge
I see both the moon
and its reflection
the past slips behind me
a dream written on water


a laughing gull
skimming the beach
at ebb tide
what the ocean leaves
for the shell seekers


the past
rising wraith-like
to color my now . . .
as Bette Midler sings *The Rose*
our ghosts go ballroom dancing


*swimming*
in the Silver River*
of stars . . .
our constellations touching
though light years apart

*~Picayune, Mississippi, USA*

*\* Note: The Silver River is a modern Chinese name for the
Milky Way, although many Chinese still prefer the richly
nuanced River of Heaven.*

# Debbie Strange

snowbound
we sip Darjeeling
and dream
of growing marigolds
in monsoon rain


drumbeats
calling down the rain
we walk
with muddy feet
petrichor on our skin


the degrees
of separation
between us
i am summer's heat
you are winter's chill


this baggage
carried from one life
to the next
we unpack everything
but our belongingness

*~Winnipeg, Manitoba, Canada*

# Joanna Ashwell

the hills
cold-packed
in silence . . .
evening wind,
sing to me


ladders to the sky
cumuli-nimbus gathers
thoughts soar
together we climb
alone we fall


chalked bicycles
Tour de France markers
etched on moorland roads
Yorkshire ruminates
where the wheels spun through


if only we could pretend
not to hear the footsteps
our house of shards
complete with splinters
might just leave us alone


your special cake
fingers knead the flour
a candle for each year
a flicker of flame quickens
beneath your breath


on this night
cold enough for snow
we count the stars
infinity
tearing us apart

*~United Kingdom*

# Chen-ou Liu

time over time
I-then and I-now
face to face
with each other . . .
my first Easter Sunday


freezing drizzle
expected to mix
with the snow
I feel the urge
to stir my coffee clockwise


I cough and roll
from one side of the bed
to the other
under my body
the shards of a past

*~Ajax, Ontario, Canada*


our first date
at her New Writing Series
over her shoulder
I whisper a tanka
yet to be published


love-struck
by her Mona Lisa smile
and eyes
that gaze upon me
yet look beyond


green light
blinking at the end
of her dock . . .
one bay, two worlds
too far apart, yet so close

*~Toronto, Ontario, Canada*


no moon, no stars
in the dead of night
loneliness
smelling of the attic . . .
another time and place

*~Ajax, Ontario, Canada*


laundry flapping
in the summer wind
a circle of men
at a communal meal
in the Alfama street

*~Lisbon, Portuguese*


single file
on the long way home:
the shadow,
myself and a man
who carries a scythe

*for Ingmar Bergman*


after 9/11
I had to shave off
my long beard . . .
the new temp tells me
with a stained-teeth smile

*~Ajax, Ontario, Canada*

# Nicholas B. Hamlin

from my hotel room
above Tokyo Bay
blue-grey morning
contradicts my excitement
I feel I am still dreaming


as the day begins
arise and smell the coffee
or else slumber on
not unlike my love
refusing to open eyes


the Edo garden
hidden from the sidewalk
by the hotel
reminds me of back home
where I go to think

~Tokyo, Japan


on the bullet train
en route to Matsumoto
I am at ease
a glimpse of Fuji
I wake my friend from his nap


ducking through tunnels
in Matsumoto Castle
I am transported
I didn't bring my camera
what else have I forgotten?

~Matsumoto, Japan


narrow tunnels
cut through Japanese alps
lens cap on
for worry of distracting
the driver in the mirror

school children waving
I am not by the window
this bus moves faster
than my thoughts at the moment
of people I know back home


watching the river
rushing
I only regret
shoes soaked
from before

~Kamikochi, Japan


two friends of a friend
meet us in Osaka
they speak English well
embarrassed by our questions
they have good answers to give


central station
a city of its own
the elevator
tests our patience
we stay on the first floor


electric bike
riding around Osaka
getting looks
delightful or confused
we return them all


more friends of friends
in a band in Osaka
they are so friendly
and tremendously funny
I hope to see them again

~Osaka, Japan

watching my drunk friend
dance to "This Must Be The Place"
I admire him
he is feeling the moment
his arms are not his own


one Kyoto night
we walk the street
through a temple
car lights flash
from the top of the stairs

*~Kyoto, Japan*


snorkeling
off the coast
an eel hides from me
retreating like my problems
no longer within my view


sunburnt
about to go on a hike
the sky is now clear
I am shedding my old skin
I am growing a new one

*~Kushimoto, Japan*

## *Sedoka*

## Bruce England


For a reporter,
Naresh Kumar of Bihar,
stops long enough to respond
"I follow the work;"
hoisting his buckets of dirt,
"I cannot afford feelings"


Two men read the book,
I will not be sad in this world,
when they met at last, one said
"what a bunch of crap"
the other said, "you still carry
that load of crap in your mind"


To be a stone
to know nothing and endure
for the longest of times
or to be human
and know just a little
for the shortest of times


Yellow sunlight
dust motes circle around
a little boy peeing
in my condo
yellow the least color
among my too many things


From Highway 1
we found the way to Bolinas
minus the turnoff sign
in motel bar
Bolinas cowboys played pool
in clean Adidas shoes

*~United States*

# Responsive Tanka Sequences

*Toward an Integration of Japanese Aesthetics and the Western Literary Tradition*

## David Rice

When poets write together, they unfailingly report how much they enjoyed the experience, but what about the reader? What kind of responsive poem is likely to engage someone who was not there at its creation? Although English-language responsive tanka poetry is evolving, the approach that poets have taken so far remains, to my ear, more connected to the Japanese aesthetic of linking and shifting than to theme development. This essay explores the possibility that if English-language responsive tanka sequences could integrate theme development with the linking and shifting inherent in the tanka form, the resulting sequences are more likely to engage readers raised on Western poetry.

**Background**

Although the first English-language tanka collection appeared almost a hundred years ago, the number of English-language tanka that have appeared in print and online has increased enormously in recent years. *Take Five: Best Contemporary Tanka, Volume 4* (2012), for example, reviewed more than one hundred and eighty venues where tanka had appeared in 2011. Examining this explosion of tanka writing, it is possible to see some trends in how English-language tanka poets have adapted the 1,200-year-old Japanese tanka aesthetic to the Western literary tradition. At first, most poets wrote five-line poems with thirty-one syllables in the form 5-7-5-7-7. Now, although English-language tanka continues to be written in five lines, and though many poets continue to follow the short-long-short-long-long pattern, most poets write in a less rigid and shorter form of approximately 20–24 syllables with no defined line lengths. Also, most English-language tanka used to include an image from nature; now many do not.

English-language tanka editors, though, did not follow the Japanese tanka tradition in their first anthologies. The Japanese Imperial anthologies were sequenced, and their compilers used a variety of techniques to connect the poems together. Until recently, most English-language anthologies—and journals—did not sequence poems, choosing instead to present the tanka alphabetically by author's name.

The broader question is what are the possibilities when adapting the tanka form to the Western poetry tradition. Brower and Miner (1961) wrote that the Japanese tanka aesthetic emphasizes implication, affect, tone, and quality of experience, while the corresponding Western aesthetic emphasizes representation, ideas, themes, and metaphors. Luxton said that for tanka to become part of mainstream English-language poetry, it needs to address and explore subjects in more detail (Leuck, 2014). I take him to mean that English-language tanka needs to include more variety and depth of ideas and themes along with the Japanese tanka aesthetic.

With respect to sequences, whether written by one poet or more than one poet, Goldstein (2010) has pointed out that there are different ways to organize them. He distinguished between tanka strings (a series of links that flow one to the other without an overall organizing principle) and tanka sequences (where a change occurs between the beginning and end). The more change, the more a sequence integrates Western poetic expectations with Japanese aesthetics.

Braniger (2011) also addressed this issue and provided examples of how she and her colleagues, writing responsive tanka (in trios and quartets), "reach beyond Goldstein's categories of 'sequence' and 'string' [. . .] toward a blended genre, which consists of an integration of the two forms [. . .] a sequence of strings" (p. 72). By connecting strings of poems, their final poems showed overall movement and change. This integration is in the direction of adding a Western literary element to the Japanese aesthetic of linking and shifting. Angela Leuck (2012), discussing different ways to approach responsive tanka, advocated that poets "tackle more difficult or controversial subjects [and] artfully incorporat [e] a narrative element" (p. 60). Although the terminology may differ, all three writers see differences in the way tanka sequences can be written.

The primary goal of English-language tanka need not be to join mainstream English-language poetry, but a lot more people read mainstream poetry than read English-language tanka. If English-language tanka poets could more fully integrate the Japanese aesthetic to the Western literary tradition, more people would be likely to read English-language tanka, and all poets want readers. Leuck (2012) wrote "bringing in our own [Western] traditions to tanka, I believe, we are extending the form [. . .] making it [. . .] more contemporary and with greater appeal to a wider current audience" (p. 60).

**Responsive Poetry**

Lovers exchanged tanka in *The Tale of Genji* (1980), written over a thousand years ago. In the 1600s Japanese poets began writing renga together. There was no focus on theme development or personal emotional exchange in renga. Instead, the form developed an elaborate set of rules for linking and shifting. English-language tanka poets focused first on writing individual tanka, but in the last ten years they have begun to explore responsive tanka sequences. For those English-language tanka poets familiar with renga, the rules for linking and shifting may have provided a foundation for writing responsive tanka.

Responsive tanka are an excellent way to integrate Western and Japanese poetry aesthetics.

A responsive tanka sequence is a poetic conversation, and conversations have meaning as well as style. Poetic responses can develop a theme in ways that an individual poet could not, just as we can say something in a conversation we had never said like that before. The Japanese aesthetic of affect and tone is a good fit for a poetic conversation. When people talk, feelings affect thoughts, and how a conversation goes depends, in many situations, on the relationship between the people involved. By adding the poets' relationship to the sequence, the sequence gains another dimension because, besides developing a theme, the poets can write to each other; the pronouns "we" and "you" can refer to the poets themselves. When Cherie Hunter Day and I wrote *Kindle of Green* (2008), for example, she responded to "though I still see them/the migrating geese/are too distant to hear/I didn't expect/to miss your voice so much" with "in a crowded cafe/I wonder what I would say/to the stranger/at the corner table/if he turned out to be you." Individual tanka linking and shifting around a theme that includes the relationship between the poets is a form that is likely to engage the reader as well as the poets.

When having a poetic conversation, poets have to solve the problem of how many lines to write. There are many possible solutions, but the shortness of the tanka form has advantages for a poetic conversation because, by forcing each poet to be succinct, the conversation keeps moving back-and-forth; getting to the point increases intimacy and intensity in any conversation.

English-language poets have been writing "collaborative" poetry for seventy years (Duhamel, Seaton, & Trinidad, 2007; Murphy & Weber, 2007), and "collaborative" is a better word than "responsive" to describe most of these poems, as far as the reader is concerned. The poems have a title and two (sometimes more than two) authors, but on the page the poems look as if they were written by one person because, in most cases, the collaboration involved the poets trading lines so that their separate voices merged into one unified voice. The poetic form where two poets respond to each other in a way that emphasizes the conversational aspect for the reader is a specific kind of collaborative poetry that English-language poets have not much explored. (However, see Bell & Stafford (1983), Harrison & Kooser (2003), and Xu & Sturm (2013).

English-language haiku poets also have a long history of linking together. Tan renga, the closest form to tanka, involves one poet writing the first 2–3 lines and another poet completing the five line poem. Poets then can link multiple tan renga together to create a sequence. Tan renga can have titles, but most of the tan renga I have seen focus more on linking and shifting than on theme-development.

## English-language Responsive Tanka Sequences

If responsive poetry is largely unexplored in the Western literary tradition, and if tanka is a good form to use when writing responsive poetry, how are English language poets integrating the Japanese linking and shifting aesthetic with the Western, more theme-focused literary tradition? One way to answer this question is to imagine a continuum, with links without a theme between the tanka at one end and theme-driven links at the other.

The first responsive sequences that English-language tanka poets wrote (which I am aware of) fell towards the Japanese aesthetic end of the line. They were organized around a subject, but in most cases the responses did not explore a theme. Instead, the sequences followed the meandering path the poets traveled as they wrote together, and the emphasis was on the linking and shifting between each tanka. However, over the past ten years responsive tanka poets have changed the way they arrange the poems on the page, title the poems, and indicate who wrote which poem.

For instance, Holley & Yuhki (2005) and Fielden & Kitaui (2008) both printed the poems one or two to a page, divided the book into titled sections, and placed the poet's name or initial with each poem. Arntzen & Walken (2010), though, had two-tanka conversations, each on their own page; they titled their sections with the poet's initial near each poem. Fielden & Ogi (2011) printed the poems two to a page in titled sections, with the poet's initials with each poem, but Fielden & Kitaui (2011) wrote a poetic diary together and printed the poems two to a page; each month was a section and each poet's poems were in a distinct typeface. George (2012), writing with friends, printed each sequence on the same page, with its own title; to distinguish who wrote each tanka, one poet's poems were italicized.

If the poems in a responsive tanka sequence appear on the same page or pages—depending on the length of the poem, the reader can more easily follow the poem's thematic development than if the individual links are on separate pages. If the poem has a title that relates to the theme, the title can help the reader follow the theme through the linking and shifting. If the poet's poems are italicized or differentiated on the page in some way, it helps the reader follow the conversation.

(Another way to write a responsive tanka sequence is to make the conversation itself the center of the sequence and not indicate which poet wrote which poem. Day & Rice (2008) and Suse & Montreuil (2013) took this approach, as did the mainstream poets Kooser & Harrison (2003), who explained "this book is an assertion in favor of poetry and against credentials.")

## Conclusion

Maybe it is fool's gold, but I see a responsive tanka poetry that places the conversation at the center of the poem, and addresses themes by linking and shifting, as a large gold nugget sitting in a field waiting for tanka poets to scoop it up. I have been prospecting for responsive tanka sequences for many years. Though not necessarily pieces of gold—flakes maybe—here are two I wrote with *Lynne Leach*

Past Perfect

> *my Sunday ritual—*
> *to wind my antique clocks—*
> *after I'm gone*
> *who will care*
> *to keep them ticking*

many blossoms
on our apple tree
again
I silently thank
whoever planted it

*a Paris spring*
*black umbrellas bob beneath*
*dripping chestnut trees*
*I've stepped into a picture*
*someone painted long ago*

on my wall
a watercolor
of a rainy graveside
impossible to read
the names on the tombstones

*cathedral ruins*
*empty window sockets frame*
*dark scudding clouds*
*where once voices rose in praise*
*now just the wind . . . then silence*

redwood grove
we whisper
in the giant presence
of the past
I don't have to worry

Beyond the linking and shifting, the theme is the relationship between us and those who were here before and, by extension, our relationship to those who will follow us when we are no longer here. Lynne focuses on "after I'm gone," I reply by "thanking" those who are now gone, she replies by imagining she lived "long ago," I reply by saying even people's names from long ago are gone, she agrees, and I add that being gone doesn't mean I have to worry. The title, "Past Perfect," refers both to how we can idealize the past and also how, if we can get past idealizing, we "don't have to worry."

Survival

*guests full of praise*
*for my house . . . trees . . . views . . .*
*until suddenly*
*termites swarm from somewhere*
*wings a red blur in the light*

the rat
in the bathroom wall
scurried for weeks
its scritch-scratching
a rake on my skull

*the oak's trunk*
*a woodpecker drilling*
*a necklace of holes*
*the wasteful spill of life-sap*
*in a ring around my feet*

two names
carved in a heart
my love
is big enough to sweeten
the whole forest

*fire blackened*
*the redwood's core*
*a gaping scar*
*this heart has survived the stress*
*of ten thousand sorrows*

meadows edge
a green tree frog hops
past a seedling
our conversations
a path to follow

The theme is how we respond to the entropy that continually affects us. Lynne reports "termites" eating her praise-worthy house, I say that has happened to me ("rat in the bathroom wall"), she says her oak tree lost "life-sap" to a woodpecker, I say sometimes change can bring unexpected sweetness, she says she has been scarred and has survived, and I say we help each other survive. The title, "Survival," refers to how we can, together, slow the inevitable pull of entropy.

I would like to thank Cherie Hunter Day, Angela Leuck, and Joan Zimmerman for their valuable comments on an earlier draft of this essay.

## References

Arntzen, S. & Walken, N.B. (2010). *Double Take: Response Tanka*. Baltimore, MD: Modern English Tanka Press.

Braniger, C. (2011). Responsive Tanka Trios & Quartets: A New Twist on Collaborative Composition. *Atlas Poetica: A Journal of Poetry and Place*, 11, 65-73.

Brower, R.H. & and Miner, E. (1961). *Japanese Court Poetry*. Stanford, CA: Stanford University Press.

Day, C.H. & Rice, D. *Kindle of Green* (2008). San Diego, CA: Platypus Books.

Duhamel, D., Seaton, M. & Trinidad, D. (Eds). (2007). *Saints of Hysteria: A Half-Century of Collaborative American Poetry*. Brooklyn, NY: Soft Skull Press.

Fielden, A. & Kitaui, K. (2008). *In Two Minds*. Baltimore, MD: Modern English Tanka Press.

Fielden, A. & Kitaui, K. (2011). *Yesterday, Today and Tomorrow*. Brisbane, Australia: Interactive Press.

Fielden, A. & Ogi, S. (2011). *Words Flower*. Brisbane, Australia: Interactive Press.

George, B. writing with Friends. (2012). *Winds Through the Wheatfields*. Self-published.

Goldstein, S. (2010). Not Again! Yes, Tanka Strings, Tanka Sequences. *Atlas Poetica: A Journal of Poetry and Place*, 5, 60-65.

Holley, A. & Yuhki, A. (2005). *White Flower in the Sky*. Printed in Japan.

Kei, M. (Editor-in-Chief). *Take Five: Best Contemporary Tanka Volume 4* (2012). Perryville, MD: Keibooks.

Kooser, T. & Harrison, J. (2003). *Braided Creek: A Conversation in Poetry*. Port Townsend, WA: Copper Canyon Press.

Leuck, A. (2012). Book Review Editor's Message: Responsive Tanka: Art and Craft. *Ribbons*, 8 (2), 59-61.

Leuck, A. (2014). Book Review Editor's Message: Tanka and the Literary Mainstream: Are We "There" Yet? *Ribbons*, 10 (1), 68-74.

Murphy, S.E. & Weber, M.L. (Eds.) (2007). *>2: An Anthology of New Collaborative Poetry*. North Charleston, SC: BookSurge Publishing.

Shikibu, M. Trans. Royall Tyler. (2001). *The Tale of Genji*. NY: Penguin Books.

Stafford, W. & Bell, M. (1983). *Seques: A Correspondence in Poetry*. Jaffrey, NH: David R. Godine Publisher.

Suse, L. & Montreuil, M. (2013). *A Hint of Light: Response Tanka*. Self-published.

Xu, W. and Sturm, N. (2013). *I Was Not Even Born*. Atlanta, GA: Coconut Books.

# Of Tanka Prose and Tanka

## Peter Fiore

Let's begin with Alice Walker's phrase "the value and beauty of the authentic"—to hit the bottom line of our aesthetics, no matter what form you are writing, short story, memoir, poem, or tanka prose. And you have to be quick. You have maybe a sentence, a line, to establish your authenticity.

Because a second aesthetic principle is brevity. No unnecessary words or attachments. Know when to stop.

I am not a scholar. I have never studied tanka or tanka prose in any formal or intense way. I sell advertising for the construction industry, teach tennis, and write a variety of short forms with my left foot. But when M. Kei asked me to write an article on tanka prose, I started reading as much as I could find. I read casually, especially during the baseball season, and this Derek Jeter's last. But the question that interests me—does tanka prose have to contain a tanka to make it tanka prose, or can the prose stand by itself as tanka prose?—was not addressed in any of the reading I have done so far.

As you can probably guess, my answer to this question is no, tanka prose does not have to contain a tanka to make it tanka prose. What then makes it tanka prose? Tanka has a certain movement and rhythm, just as a sonnet has its movement, just as haiku, and blues have theirs. Rhythm in tanka is established by its breaks. There can be breaks at the end of each line or as Sanford Goldstein has suggested it can be "a rush of five lines down." We can easily point to other qualities of tanka: its lyricism, its use of imagery, its clarity and indirection. But it's the movement of tanka prose that defines it best.

Here's tanka prose by Marilyn Morgan:

### House Plants

I have several plants scattered throughout the house and among my favorites are a few African violets. This morning I looked with great surprise at the ones sitting on the bed stand.

It's been a hot summer and usually by this time of year, my plants need some loving attention. I'm away most of the summer so plants are left to fend for themselves. Yet the leaves of this violet were healthy—a vibrant green, crisp and strong. No blossoms or even buds, though. Dormant as if waiting my return.

And then as if to greet me, I saw the awakening.

Two adjacent stems in the center of this violet stood straight upright, tall and sturdy, each with a full healthy leaf leaning against the other.

If I didn't know better, I'd say they were fucking.

Say what you like, this is written "in the spirit of tanka." Would the inclusion of a tanka poem make this any more tanka prose? I don't think so. It would in fact clutter and seem tacked on. Here's another originally published in *Still Crazy*:

### Before Entering the Gorges

Free ballets of sun on the water like rim shots, soundless underwater landscapes drift under the raft.

All afternoon whole choruses of silence.

We inspect the shallows where the bottom shimmers between patches of algae like the golden streets of ancient Mexican cities and grass sways to the rhythm of water.

The fish look transparent.

They swim out of the shadows, suck insects skating on the surface, vanish into patches of sun, and then we spot them gliding through smoky green and brown weeds, rising from farther down than we can see.

The long-short pattern of breaks contributes to what it feels like to read tanka prose. Here's an example of tanka prose that employs the-rush-of-five-lines pattern:

## Hudson River School Romantic Landscape

you can still see horses in the morning in mountain fields grazing across the street from where I live and frost on the tips of golden rod and rock walls and sun breaking through burnished trees and back in the corners abandoned hayers, field rakes and automobiles of a dead age rusting in the flowering marijuana.

This next one is more dramatic, but its subject matter gives it a lyrical twist:

## Round Midnite

you wait an extra hour and when I don't show think you're making a fool of yourself . . .

I tell you I didn't expect you to be waiting and so, when I was late, just looked quickly

and then walked to the subway without searching for you further. still we look at each other

out of this first taste of sorrow and hold hands across a table against the heartache sure to come—

"I love you," you say, "and already it hurts"

Bob Lucky has suggested that tanka prose is a form that is still evolving, that it "constantly defines and redefines itself." I offer my own tanka prose pieces, enclosed, as examples of that evolution.

## Born Again

David and Tami took Sarah everywhere. Changed and nursed her at the beach or at Felix's before dessert, and once at the L.A. County Airport where Jessaline and I'd flown in to get our first look.

She was still only two months old, my first grandchild.

She smiled and slobbered and Jessaline changed her diaper and helped Tami give her a shower and learned to hold her on her hip swaying back and forth like a palm tree, sang lullabies to her, and when it was time to leave she almost forgot her doll, Tina, crumpled in the corner of Sarah's room.

I'd brought pictures of David at that age so Tami could see the similarities and David showed me a picture of Nonna, holding me up to the camera the same age as Sarah that was like a three dimensional negative that took 48 years to develop.

But it wasn't till I was back home, driving to work that it finally hit me—like all the lights of New York City—that I'd been born again and was going to live forever. I slowed down and hung onto the steering wheel for dear life. If I'd been on a horse, it would have knocked me out of the saddle.

—first published in *Sandy River Review*

Now for a complete non-sequitur. This from M. Kei's introduction to *Take Five*, volume 4: "'Gogyohka' is a Japanese form derived from tanka, but it abandons the syllable count of traditional tanka. Gogyohka are written in five lines with due considerations for breath and aesthetics, but no requirements for the number of syllables. Although tanka and gogyohka in Japanese are quite different from each other, gogyohka and tanka in English are indistinguishable." If tanka can be written in one line as it originally was in Japan, in three lines as the tanka poets of the Naturalist School did, in four lines as Jun Fujita did, or in five lines as most tanka poets do, then why can't it be written in prose? Let's listen to Matsukaze in the Summer, 2014, edition of *Atlas Poetica*: ". . . I would humbly submit that five lines is not what makes tanka, tanka; but its musicality/rhythm, and its fiveness—five poetic phrases/segments/thought-parts . . ." (P. 75)

I rest my case.

But let's try one more because it's a little further out there. This one's not even brief, but I think it still works. Maybe because its quickness makes it brief.

## Puerto Rican Honeymoon

at Las Croabas a huge white hotel on the top of a hill with green acres of a golf course leading up to it, overlooking the sea. a metallic sculpture of Ponce de Leon guards the entrance with his lance held high and the people live below in the crowded barrios. latino chants and drums bombalading from latticed windows, plants hang on porches, dogs defeated by the heat on sidewalks, women and children on the porch, men hang out together on the streets of red Poinciana blossoms in front of the little stores. nothing has changed here in 400 years.

we wait in Ponce in a gleaming hotel for magic to arrive, some treasure we find occasionally within ourselves recognized on the throbbing streets of a coastal people waiting by the sea—prospecting for shells—for the sea to reclaim us. if you find a pearl, you get to keep it.

in the grass frogs ring coqui, there are pigeons in my breast. everything uncared for festers, around my neck is a black hand on a gold chain, around the lobby are dead women waiting to be fucked, gilded windows and satin promises. between here and Condado is a revolution. police on slick and elegant horses along the beach—a jet fighter buzzes the palm trees, banks along the cove . . . the blue infinity trembles, thunders like a whole city crashing. past before it's present, and then the wind returns.

on the beach of our birth chango birds in the palms weep like cats at sunset, at sunrise, welcome our fellowship like Indians welcoming Ponce de Leon to this green island.

I believe in poetry, in the blood of our fathers. I talk to you as I would a cloud—once again drunken kings throw money on the table. behind bars is a star. the sea flickers between condominiums, the plaza is filled with mushroom trees, the playa is filled with beer cans—a confluencia of sun and white buildings. like mirrors the sun flashes the sea slowly throbs as we roll and tumble and come up on the sand ebbing . . . in the soft night, in our little room, morning finds us tangled, like seaweed.

Tanka prose raises the question of the difference between tanka prose and microfiction, flashes, and prose poems. It's a question I don't care to address at this point. In the end, the proof is in the pudding. Does the piece move you? Do you want to read more?

## Works Cited

Lucky, Bob. "25 Tanka Prose. Introduction: TP or not TP, That is the Question." Perryville, MD: Keibooks, Spring, 2011.

Kei, M., 'Introduction: The Pity of Things.' *Take Five, Volume 4*. Perryville, MD: Keibooks, 2012.

Kusakabe, Enta. *Gogyohka*. Translated by Matthew Lane and Revised by Elizabeth Phair. Tokyo, Japan: Shisei-sha. 2009.

Matsukaze. "Tanka in Three Lines." *Atlas Poetica*. Summer, 2014, pp. 74-76.

Walker, Alice. *You Can't Keep A Good Woman Down*. Orlando, Florida: Harcourt Brace Jovanovich, 1981.

Woodward, Jeffrey. *Another Garden*. Detroit, Michigan: Tournesol, 2013.

# Odyssey of a Solitary Poet:
# A Review of M. Kei's tanka journal, *January*

## Reviewed by Charles D. Tarlton

I

*there is beauty*
*even in sadness*

Beyond observations of the vaguest generality, it would seem to be impossible accurately to characterize a work of 640 individual tanka, but *January*, M. Kei's recent tanka journal, contains that many. They are organized formally into chapters representing the twelve months of the year, although the tanka are not distributed evenly: there are 114 in January, 105 in May, 65 in April and October, 47, 42, 47, 43 in March, June, July, and December, respectively, 25 in February and August, 29 in September, and only 12 in November. We could merely remark that the tanka represent daily and personal moments across the year, quote a few of the most memorable ones, and let it go at that. And, many of the tanka here would be amenable to that; they are quick momentary takes on something witnessed, remembered, or imagined. There are tanka about mornings and evenings, about birds, the scent of wild vines, the sea, the bay, the weather, about stray cats, trees and flowers and falling leaves, failed love, and so on.

But, there is also something larger at work in *January*. Scattered across the text, we find tanka that, whatever their topical focus, mainly express sadness, pessimism, loneliness, loss, and the peculiar frustrations of unsatisfied love. In some ways, we might even read these hundreds of separate tanka as parts of a long, involved, winding sequence on resignation. The mood that predominates *January* and that makes itself clearly known from the outset is negative. This pessimistic motif is present throughout the book, but can be seen with some clarity in the

vocabulary choices Kei has made right across the first chapter, "January." Consider the weight of these recurring and typical key terms: "shame, hurts, coffin, despair, inadequacy, alone, gloomy, worries, melancholy, dying, hollow, desperate, pessimism, captive, wounded, dust and ashes, black, mortal, sadness, weeds, weary, devastation, grief, sadden . . ." And then last, but not least, there is this:

the entire sky
a threnody in grey,
a Whistler painting
without a sound,
not even birdsong

"Threnody" names a lament, from the Greek for *wailing* and *song*, and in many ways a large part of the tanka in the whole of *January*, lamenting as they do, reflect this burden of sadness, disillusionment, and sorrow.

raw and painful
this old blister;
if only our hurts
would change with
the calendar

Before concluding too much from all this, however, I think it is necessary to point out that Kei's tanka are often at the same time quite beautiful and well-wrought. Here is a tanka of sadness, but a sadness typically relieved somewhat by art.

it's a day like any other,
full of melancholy
pessimism,
and yet—somewhere
there are herons

Such achievement is evident wherever you turn in *January*. There is plenty of sadness, of course, but we are more often than not provided with the irony, pathos, humor, and beauty necessary to allow us to look to directly into the sadness without becoming dejected ourselves. Here are four tanka: note how their unquestioned darkness is relieved by poetic twists that enlarge their contexts, allowing the reader to transcend and neutralize some of the tragedy.

a few dark figures
under a dagger moon
huddle together
beneath the overpass
and passing time

the color of hope—
pink magnolia trees
blooming
against the windows
of the veterans hospital

Chesapeake night
in the middle of it,
one skipjack,
moths fluttering
around her masthead light

an elderly friend
slips into his dotage,
in the distance
a fast moving freight train
leaves this town behind

Because the book, as a tanka journal, is perforce about time, we should also be alert to just what the poet thinks about the passage of time, and the idea that most consistently comes to the fore is—*decay*. The passing of the days, the months, and the years constitute no romantic trope for Kei, but amount to a corrosive force that wears down the best hopes and intentions. Here is his entry for the fulcrum date of December 31 (the last day of the year and of the book, and the day just before the first day of the next year— "In my beginning is my end?"). They are his last words on the subject.

last night
of the year—
another
set of hopes
abandoned

This is a book, then, mainly about disappointment, high expectations abandoned, about longing, and about various kinds of death —the real ones, when mothers and fathers and friends actually die,

a green valley
but my mother bleeding
red, red, so red
these are the secret things
a child never forgets

the memory
comes unexpectedly,
I wonder
if there was very much
blood when he died

and the symbolic ones, the death of dreams or hope,

Saturday morning—
a crow
picking at
the breadcrumbs of
my existence

there was a time
when I had faith in
a better future;
now it is enough to
breathe ordinary air

One of the saddest aspects of *January* might just be the idea that the clearest responsibility for hope, from season to season, rests with the birds.

> it's because of January
> that God made cardinals;
> when our hearts are weary
> of the long grey cold
> and we yearn for spring

> first birdsong of the year
> somewhere,
> amid all the brown gloom,
> a small life is
> happy to greet the day

The memories of love and sex are among the most poignant of the recurring topics in *January*, and, again, there is very little that we might call uplifting in this discussion. Love, in the sense of true love, seems but the remotest possibility, as the tanka focus on nostalgia and regret. There are gay tanka recalling past same-sex encounters, but there is little mention here of lasting relationships or anything we might connect to romantic love. Here are some examples.

> there is nothing
> quite so delightful
> as someone
> eager to learn
> all my vices

> it was a shock
> to see his name again
> and feel
> my queerness awake
> after silence

> his relatives don't like him,
> so he tells them
> he's sleeping with
> a famous male poet
> twice his age

> Queen Cardinal
> in your dowager weeds,
> why do so many
> brilliant males court you,
> but never me?

> throwing away
> old papers,
> I found a love letter—
> I vaguely recall
> that boy-man

> I wanted to argue,
> but the sandpaper of
> his jaw
> was more than my
> lips could resist

The situation with respect to more conventional love and marriage offers little added consolation. Broken marriage provides the background and is the source of lingering ill feelings as Kei finds things that here and there remind him of the wreckage. Here is a sampling.

> married
> to the tune of 'Greensleeves,'
> now divorced,
> "Alas my love,
> you do me wrong."

> ten years
> since she married
> someone else;
> why does it bother me
> to forget her birthday?

> Bridal Veil Falls—
> I saw them as a child
> two divorces later
> they remain a vision
> never quite forgotten

> reading a book
> of someone else's
> love poems,
> I sigh a little and
> turn to the dawn

one bagpipe
in a mist-filled dawn—
that was the sound
of a lover's hopes
unfulfilled

I haven't had
a broken heart in years
it's an accomplishment
that leaves me
feeling a little sad

Finally, as you might expect, there are purely seasonal tanka in every chapter, tanka marking the change from winter to spring and from summer to autumn, although it would be fairer to say that each season is more enjoyed in the anticipation than in the arrival, as the poet looks forward to change only to find that nothing, really, has changed. Winter makes him long for spring, but spring's thaw only reveals the destruction hidden under snow and ice.

in the mud
next to the asphalt,
a broken doll's head,
a crow pecking
at plastic eyes

## II

there's poetry
in everything, even
in the fear
at the top of
a swaying mast

As we have seen, there are themes or patterns across Kei's year of tanka writing. Nevertheless, the 640 individual tanka remain mostly discrete and stand-alone. We can imagine the poet at the end of each day sorting through the scribbled notes he has been shoving into his pockets and choosing the best ones to copy out and refine. The tanka serve as a kind of window on the poet's life and state of mind, separating those days when he spent a lot of time musing poetically from the days when he was otherwise busy, and harvested only one or two tanka (or none). On at least two major occasions, however, the poet has created elaborate and extended tanka sequences; first, in a sensitive narrative of a five-day boat trip on the Chesapeake Bay at the end of October; and, second, in accounts of two naturalist hikes along a path in the woods, one undertaken in May and the second, the follow-up, in December. We know from Kei's other writings that talk of boats is, for him, important talk, so we'll start there.

*All at Sea*

Beginning near the end of January, nautical tanka start to be sprinkled along the way to what will be the centerpiece cruise on the skipjack *Martha Lewis*. These early ones, despite being about boats, border on the morose, probably a result of the short days and long nights.

her screw
still turning as she
went down,
the *Sarah C. Conway*,
dead at 114

it hurts to know
so many bones of
dead vessels
lie in watery tombs
beneath my feet

all silted up,
the Elk River will
never know
another gull-winged
schooner

could there be
anything sadder to see
than an old schooner,
her sails wung out,
hogbacked and grey?

In February, winter continues to take its toll. The poet is glad, on the one hand, that he doesn't "have to sail / these bitter waters," but in the very next tanka he tells us,

> I miss the boat
> crave it
> the water
> the herons
> and the world

Mentions of boats continue to be gloomy till the end of February where the last mention of ships that month amounts to a kind of ghost story.

> the *Sarah C. Conway*
> sinking through a hole
> in the storm . . .
> what spirits flew out
> of this white world?

By March, however, we begin to hear of actual work on the boat, even though it seems to be about the most routine maintenance.

> crawling into the bilge,
> the wood still damp even
> in the middle of winter,
> the cold wind blowing
> through her seams

> winter maintenance
> two hours after
> I crawl out of the bilge
> of an old boat,
> my butt's still cold

On April 1, still more maintenance as the poet and his son are applying Copperkote to the boat's bilge, but he still manages to tie the labor to some disquieting reflections.

> a book of poetry later,
> my hands still
> smell like this afternoon's
> Copperkote and
> the bilge of an old boat

> my son and I
> crawl through the bilge
> of an old wooden boat,
> painting Copperkote
> for another fifty years

> ladled out of
> mother's womb,
> I continue to
> splatter and spill
> this life of mine

And, again, on April 6, along with his son and daughter, the poet is back to tarring the boat against leaks and corrosion, stripping metal parts for refinishing, and making poetry out of the work.

> scooting in the sawdust
> beneath the boat,
> my son holds the flashlight
> while I tar the inside
> of the centerboard well

> sitting on a stack of lumber,
> my daughter strips the paint
> from a piece of
> metal hardware
> to be restored to the boat

> anointed
> with tar after working
> on the boat,
> I take a bath in WD-40
> and come out slick and clean

> one spot of tar
> I didn't remove—
> a tattoo of
> winter work
> upon my skin

Tanka about the boat become more concentrated as we go forward, and we can sense the poet's growing eagerness for some kind of voyage to start. On October 4, 10, and 13, there are tanka that suggest that it may, in fact, have already started.

outsailed
by a monarch butterfly
whose small wings
will carry him
all the way to Mexico

drowned island
beneath our keel,
if I reach down
will I find a hand
reaching up?

dinner begins
with a safety talk:
in the event of emergency,
pull the ceiling knobs
for life jackets

Nevertheless, the tanka boat trip proper has begun by October 17 and goes on for 14 pages and 5 days in the journal. This may be the point of sharpest and most intense focus in the whole of *January*. The morning of departure:

a raft of waterfowl
vague
in the morning mist
the red disk of the sun
the only color

the muffled thump
of artillery as we pass
the proving ground,
fog, water, and dawn,
mute in the autumn morning

the rising sun
finally
strong enough
to warm my face
this autumn morning

You can feel the deck underfoot, see the sails fill in the wind, the boat lean into its turn. Then we're sailing up the bay. The shore glides past and the poet/sailor notes their position.

the first range marker
the faintest trace
of Poole Island
low in the fog
behind it

This is, we are reminded, not a pleasure boat, but a working oyster boat out among the other working boats.

work day on the Bay:
a barge
steaming south,
a crab boat
working her lines

a work day
in autumn—
no pleasure boats
on these
cold waters

a pleasure boat
never knows the Bay
like an oysterboat does,
with winter looming
behind the horizon

As the boat moves out into the bay, the focus shifts back to the poet/sailor again, this time at the helm, the day's work in front of him.

meandering south
at the helm of
the *Martha Lewis*,
the number of pleasure boats
increases with the temperature

Anyone who has ever been on even a tourist cruise in inland waters, a sight-seeing boat ride on the San Francisco Bay, say, crossing from Seattle to Victoria on a ferry, or a sail around Narragansett Bay, has had the same feeling; the docks and buildings behind you fall away and the expanse of sea slides toward you, under you, and past the boat to come out behind in the spreading wake. Here, the poet watches the Chesapeake Bay traffic under the bridge and we feel the expanse of it, the vitality.

center span
of the Bay Bridge
all courses converge—
tugs, freighters,
skipjacks, powerboats

the deadrise
*Shameless*
zooms past with
her Virginia bow
in the air

Bay Bridge—
I've been under it
more times
than I've been
over it

*Woodwind II*
in full sail,
blue pennon
snapping in
the breeze

the rusty red silhouette
of Bloody Point Light,
the white hull of a
deadrise skimming
past its base

The poet's boat passes "shore houses / still dark beneath / rose and amber clouds," and out into the middle of the Bay. The "Holland Island Bar Light / shrinking astern," we are soon in the middle of the Chesapeake Bay, "empty / but for / one skipjack," and the beam sea hitting the boat sideways sends a "spray / indistinguishable from / the first drops of rain."

a fair day
in the offing,
mackerel clouds
and a mellow sea
in an autumn dawn

a hunting pelican
the brown and white
flash of wings
skimming low
over the water

off Janes Island
a pair of pelicans
skimming the water
faster than
our motor can push

These pages are filled with tanka that aim to capture the feeling of being on the water, the world seen from that odd angle, and the life out there—boats darting to and fro, smoke from a wildfire drifting over the water, vistas of Baltimore in the distance, and that butterfly comes back into the picture.

pleasure boats
on the Severn River
the last
monarch butterfly
of the season

And, then, it is over. The boat comes about for its return trip.

passing Poole Island
the first range light appears—
in the home stretch,
I long for a hot shower
in my own house

*Through the Woods* (May 6, 2007)

This hike in the woods will be no romantic romp, no genteel picnic, and no delicate verse recited against a landscape by Gainsborough. This is the twenty-first century and this is Maryland—

trash tells me
that other feet have
trod this trail,
but today
I am the first

Nevertheless, at the outset there are birds and the promise of a fuller spring to come. The mosses are green before the trees, the briar roses have not yet bloomed as the poet moves out of the woods, across a clearing, and back into "cool green shadows— / the path less traveled / has made all the difference," when, suddenly,

> outside the wall of green,
> an unwelcome voice,
> car horns, traffic,
> the sound of my own feet,
> and then the sighing of the wind

and then Kei gives us this rude contrast,

> woodland hiking—
> the earth still chill,
> the youngest shades
> of green being born,
> heralded by the birds

> shining like a mirror:
> the end of a discarded
> beer can
> before the weeds
> cover it

There are sad signs in the woods of the failed attempt by someone to make a home—splintered planks along the path, broken glass, rusty nails, a vine covered chain link fence, and, then this mysterious find (ominous for its tying up together of pollution and progress);

> an orange stake
> labeled "control point"
> flagged with
> blue and white ribbons
> in the middle of the woods

> discarded soda cans,
> "Moon Mist" flavor
> next to the stake
> that calls itself
> "control point"

Let me digress here for just a moment. When I was a boy in southern California, we lived amongst glorious navel orange groves. My brother and I happily hunted, played, and stole from them. One day, all over the grove behind our house we discovered lath-stakes with little ribbons stapled to their tops—surveyors' markers for the bulldozers that came next and reduced the orange trees to bonfires and paradise to tract housing. I could be wrong here about what Kei is describing, but I recognize clearly the stab inside the chest.

Quickly, however, the sequence comes to an end on the perfect metaphor, an image that sums up the hike's underlying motif. As the poet emerges from the woods, he discovers that a car has apparently killed a deer and its corpse lies beside the highway. I don't think I could add anything to what Kei provides in the following six tanka.

> *memento mori*—
> the white bones
> of a deer
> slowly sinking
> into the loam

> hollow ribs,
> empty of marrow,
> hollow vertebrae,
> empty of will,
> all things come to this

> no skull nor pelvis,
> but an empty soda bottle
> where a heart should be,
> the bones disturbed
> before I ever found them

> the remains
> of another dead deer—
> the stench drives me back
> to view gnawed legbones
> and a torn pelt

> a nest of dead grass
> where the doe first lay,
> her legbones torn away
> and licked clean by
> something hungry

those first bones
were so very small—
without the dead doe
I would have never
known the fawn

As the poet steps out of the woods, his eyes fall upon sweet wild flora,

a bramble rose
snags my sleeve—
a reminder of
this living world
about to bloom

five
creamy white petals
the first briar rose
blooms
beside my boot

and seals the memory up his imagination.

dead deer
and white blooms—
this is a thing
I will not
soon forget

He turns for home, then, but the forest resists him.

clumps of
yellow blooming weeds
in this field
it is I am who am
useless and unwanted

I want to go home now—
this forest no longer
gives me passage,
brambles and deadfalls
block my way

thorns grab
my clothes and
hold me back,
but a rock
offers me a place to rest

"[P]erhaps I shouldn't leave," he wonders to himself, but then he spies the clumsy trail his heavy boots have made and turns to "follow myself back / to whence I came." I can envisage the poet safely at home, grateful and a little sad now that his walk of discovery in the woods is over.

my black boots
still in the shower,
drying off
after hiking
through the woods

*Through the Woods* (Reprise: December 3, 2007)

At the end of the year, in the midst of winter, the poet returns to his path in the woods, the path that had been so difficult in the thick greenness of spring.

the path
that was once
shut up
by summer's green gates
is now open

Winter reveals even more human detritus, but somehow neutralizes much of the threat that had been there in spring— "the control point . . . meaning even less / under a hawk wind." Winter has taken its toll, leaves are gone or withered, wind has replaced the earlier blooms, and then he arrives at the place where the deer had died.

this is the place
where the dead doe lay
last spring—
nothing left but
a huddle of broken bones

a little fur
surrounding empty
eye sockets,
the rest of her
picked clean

The wood is a constantly changing place, and you could never walk it twice, the poet says. The decay of winter is everywhere visible, "the dying wood / winter weak / past its autumn glory." The poet sits on the same stone he had visited in May, feeling less fearful than he had, and finds that now he is reluctant to leave.

the woods
that seemed impenetrable
in summer
are hollow in
December's wind

But, the thinning of the leaves and resulting greater visibility are, in the end, only sad. The reader is left with the premonition that, in the long run, even this wood, made significant by the poet's "explorations," will fall to the same march of civilization that corrupts all that is historical and valuable in the poet's beloved Chesapeake.

another stake
that calls itself
"control point"
the sound of garbage cans,
the barking of dogs

last year's
discarded Christmas trees
needles faded
at last to
the color of straw

III

Looking back over *January* and venturing on a last sort of assessment, I would like to say only two things. First of all, and I think even Kei would agree with this, there are too many tanka here for them all to be in the front rank. Had the book been shortened simply by removing the weakest tanka, it would have created a more powerful impression. It is difficult, I think, to sustain a high level of interest when a fantastic tanka, one with balance, punch, and language, is then followed by another or several that seem

hardly thought out at all.

Second, and this is not so much a criticism as an observation about tanka writing in general. To the western poetic ear, I believe, tanka are far too short to make strong and lasting impact except in the rarest cases. It is one thing to imagine that when one is writing tanka in English one somehow enters upon the Japanese tradition, but even there, I would argue (and admittedly, my knowledge here is limited) that even the most effective Japanese tanka are those wrapped up in exchanges among poets, in sequences, and in works that combine poetry with prose. I believe that the sequences in *January* on sailing and woodland hikes are effective, but I also think they (and a good deal of the tanka material in *January*) could have been made more significant and memorable had they been integrated with the occasional prose package, especially in tanka prose that might have been used further to explore the boundaries of that genre. Whenever I read individual tanka my sensibility looks around for the missing prose passage that might have rooted them more richly in an idea.

Finally, and only partly seriously, there ought to have been some kind of acknowledgement (if only for the reader perhaps new to poetry) of the debt owed to William Carlos Williams and his 'Asphodel, That Greeny Flower.'

Here is Kei's tanka;

it is difficult
to get the news from poems,
but every day
men kill for the lack
of what is found there

and then Williams;

It is difficult
to get the news from poems
yet men die miserably every day
for lack
of what is found there.

Charles D. Tarlton
San Francisco, California

# Review : *Hedgerows, Tanka Pentaptychs*

## Reviewed by Patricia Prime

*Hedgerows: tanka pentaptychs*
by Joy McCall, edited by M. Kei
Keibooks, USA, 2014
Kindle: $5.00 / Pb. 119 pp. Price: $11.70
ISBN: 978-0692200988

In his introduction to *Hedgerows,* M. Kei explains the way in which he first became aware of McCall's writing:

> It has been two years since Canadian poet Lynda Monahan submitted a tanka sequence with Joy McCall for publication in my journal *Atlas Poetica: A Journal of Poetry of Place in Contemporary Tanka.* In the wake of that acceptance, Joy was emboldened to send her own submission featuring tanka about her city of Norwich in England.

M. Kei ends his Introduction by saying:

> This time, Joy has written and collected ninety-five tanka pentaptychs (short sequences of five tanka) to form *Hedgerows: Tanka Pentaptychs.* The result is an intensely personal journey through the country within and around her.

These ninety-five pentaptychs cover a wide variety of topics from witches, ghosts, pubs, graveyards, martyrs to monkey gods and more.

On opening Joy McCall's collection, one is struck by its materiality: for a volume of such spare tanka, it is a lengthy book of 119 pages. The sense of the material is evident also in the impression made by the nostalgic photo of the ancient church and graveyard on the cover.

This reflective shading for a world displaced by the way we represent and know it, is over to

McCall's attention to the paradox of knowledge about the ancient way of life and the new. At times these edges are shown to be beautifully contingent, at other times they are revealed as oppositions. A poem like McCall's 'animus' expresses something of this paradox of knowing. I quote the first two verses:

> I know him
> the dark-skinned man
> waiting there
> his footprints crossing
> the tide-wet sand
>
> when I am distant
> he hunches in the cave
> arms around his knees
> looking out to sea
> missing my voice

The poem asks us to consider ourselves as part of something deeper—the figures, signs and sounds we use to bracket the world for knowing and sharing. We also hear this in 'sanctuary,' where we experience the knowing and not-knowing of the world:

> it was years
> before I grew
> too tall to hide
> and he took me
> into the old house
>
> and dawn came . . .
> and long dawns after
> and I watched
> from the high window
> a bird, nesting on the shed

For McCall, the instance of knowledge is haunted by its moment of presentation; the volume's tone is thus that of mystery, suspense and reflection. The poems find time to reflect on both the material and spiritual life: the experience of illness and the knowledge of one's mortality. In 'brown,' for example, we see the poet yearning and aching for the "brown of earth":

my yearning
for the brown of earth
never ends—
my skin, my flesh, my bones
pulled by the dark soil

a brown aching
for the land, the rocks,
the grainy sand
scratched with hawthorn spikes
my blood runs brown

The simple seeming poems become lessons in looking, listening, and admiring. The poems enquire into the rudiments of knowledge and the desire for synthesis:

the wind blows
from the far north hills
and I am lost—
chamomile and sage
cannot calm this longing

rosemary oil
in the jade burner
grows warm—
will it make me remember
what I would rather forget?

If there is something nostalgic, perhaps even melancholic about McCall's text, this might be due to the poet's paraplegia as a result of a motorcycle accident and her ongoing pain and fear that she might be losing her mind. The memories these poems inhabit are simultaneously hers, but this is the human paradox—even our own knowledge is not our own; we may all have experienced some of the pain and suffering that McCall writes about. She calls on, speaks to, and may speak for, other voices and other times. 'threads' is expressive of the poet coming recovering in hospital:

I sleep
the doctors come
with needles
and serious faces
and bad news

In the densities of these seemingly simple pentaptychs, we witness a fearless imagination at work: the volume's energy, its great offering, is its conviction in experience, its faith in its observations. *Hedgerows* is full of interest, as well as a good deal of humour, but is at its best in communicating the beauty of nature with impressive acuity, as we see in 'directions':

you can
find your way home
in spite of the storm
with the loud thunder
and heavy rain

by the beech tree
that stands alone
turn left
touch the bark as you pass
it is a lonely tree

McCall dedicates one of her poems, 'over the hills' to M. Kei. In contrasting stanzas she writes of herself on a 'sabbath morning' in 'the meeting-house,' while thinking of M. Kei writing "of wings and sails / of sky and sea."

On each page of McCall's volume, our all-too-human compulsion for synthesis, via knowledge, is apparent. Poem after poem attests to this compulsion by the very weight of learning, knowing and naming each evinces, and with the kind of enthusiasm that is both self-generating and evangelical; but such a positive energy, given the poet's extreme pain and confinement to a wheelchair, is outstanding. In 'devil,' for example, she is offered a pact by the devil:

the devil
showed up again
out of the blue
and offered me a deal
he thought I'd take

*one year*
he said, *as you were*
*before the crash*
*and then you die*
*finite, the end*

If this poem calls out to us, it does so in a powerful and sympathetic manner.

In lines like these from 'heather,' McCall achieves an arresting and startlingly simple beauty as she writes about her ancestors:

> my ancestors
> worked here once
> at the forge
> learning to make the weapons
> the claymore, the thin dirk

> they fought
> in these wild hills
> and were banished
> *do you hear them die,*
> *iron splitting skin?*

With passion, McCall becomes aware in these poems of the materiality of the body, the tenderness of the spirit, the joy in nature and in communicating with others. Her journey through life possesses a universal meaning that will inspire her readers.

# Review: *A Solitary Woman: tanka* by Pamela A. Babusci

## Reviewed by Patricia Prime

*A Solitary Woman: tanka*
Pamela A. Babusci
Pb. 92 pp. (2013)
To purchase a copy email the author at moongate44@gmail.com

Pamela A. Babusci is an internationally award-winning haiku/tanka poet and haiga artist. She is the founder and the editor of *Moonbathing: a journal of women's tanka*. The collection of tanka, *A Solitary Woman*, has cover art by David DeKock and an introduction by David Terelinck.

For Babusci, a woman's life can be a powerful prism, and it gives her the freedom to explore all aspects of her life: passion, sorrow, relationships, art, prayer and much more. It is an enlightening experience to read these varied aspects of one person's life.

The poet enables her readers to eavesdrop on her innermost thoughts; those between casual throw-away lines such as 'memorizing your face' to the more tightly wrapped language and energy of the title tanka:

> a solitary woman
> knows a heartache
> or two
> tossing scarlet petals
> into her evening bath

When you enter, on tiptoe, Pamela Babusci's poetic world, you might feel as if you were stepping into an oxymoronic world: one of snow and ice contrasted with that of heat and passion. An apparently contradictory intention quickly develops with a basic rule of nature:

> you have given me
> diamonds pearls
> & lavish flowers
> still a piece of your heart
> that's inaccessible

The poet seems to be divided between these two calls: the call of nature and the call of human nature. And this apparent incompatibility is at once turned into a symmetry as the poet/artist concentrates on her painting:

> putting a brush
> into paint & paint
> onto canvas
> i express my feelings
> in variations of blue

Such perfect specular symmetry is there to reinforce the trope that is the basic element of Babusci's tanka: when you are surrounded with painting and poetry or echoes of yourself you cannot know which one of these is the real you; the world of the imagination or that of reality.

Babusci finds her depth of emotion and experience in the art of writing tanka. Even in the devastating experience of her sister's miscarriage, the poet is able to find consolation:

> cutting
> turquoise-blue hyacinths
> the color of sky
> i visit my sister
> who just miscarried

But depth finds its real power when Babusci turns to painting. We understand what fascinates her in art when she says,

> a van Gogh
> starry night
> i load
> my paintbrush with his
> torment & despair

She is fascinated by the yin and yang. The real problem being, as she says in a later tanka, "you can never remove / all my childhood wounds".

In a lengthy section of tanka about her mother, Babusci writes about a complex relationship which she expresses in words which may resonate with many readers:

> never living up
> to mother's
> expectations
> now, i visit her grave
> in silence

In the tanka:

> you embrace me
> as if we'll never
> embrace again
> the moon slowly sets
> on a field of poppies

Babusci manifests her strong sense of human nature versus nature. In the anti-religious tanka:

> questioning
> God's existence
> i throw my rosary
> against the bedroom wall
> without guilt

Her persona takes out her rage against religion by becoming violent. Babusci relates to one of poetry's oldest functions which is to translate action into poetry so that it becomes a measure of future change. She uses a style that in its diction, rhythm and phonological quality reminds one of ancient Japanese women poets and their poetry.

In her section about cancer, Babusci captures the reality of the illness from its diagnosis, chemo, falling hair, to post-cancer. It's a remarkable journey that any woman, thus afflicted, would benefit by reading.

Lastly, in the collection, is a sequence of tanka about love, or lack of love:

> giving
> back the ring
> taking
> back my heart
> April rain

What one must admire about Babusci's tanka, is her honesty about her own reactions. She tells us about the fact that she is barren, that, in middle life, she is 'motherless, fatherless / childless', that she is 'betrayed by a friend', passion is fading, and much more. It's honest. She's not saintly, not all-knowing, wise, and patient—she's human, flawed.

# Review: *This Short Life: Minimalist Tanka* by Sanford Goldstein

## Reviewed by Patricia Prime

*This Short Life: Minimalist Tanka*
Sanford Goldstein
Keibooks, USA, 2014
Pb. 164 pp.
ISBN: 978-1494845599

Sanford Goldstein's new collection, *This Short Life*, is concerned with gathering tanka from a notebook he kept in 2008. He calls these tanka minimalist poems. As he explains in his Introduction:

Each poem, he says, "comes from something in my experience, in my feelings, in my memory, in my past or future."

The collection includes poems on 'Kids', 'Minimalist Sexuality', 'Nature', 'Cleanliness, Whiteness, Purity, Death', 'Food, Drinks', 'Zen, God, Faith, Doubt', 'Minimalist Tanka Humor' and 'Minimalist Multitudes'. As the titles suggest, all of the tanka included are concerned with the lived life of a man pondering his long life and what the future might hold.

The book is written by a poet between two cultures: Japan where Goldstein lives and worked in for many years, and the USA which is a space of family and heritage. *This Short Life* is a book about the power of memory, the loss of loved ones, and the questions that surround mortality.

The key tanka of the first section, 'Kids', emphasizes the theme of celebration with his family:

last night
chocolate
with almonds
before the set
with my end-of-exam kid and me

As Goldstein reflects on his children in tanka that are sometimes joyful, others miserable, or pleasurable and several conjuring suffering:

all day
my fear
of rebuke,
what it might do
to my sensitive kid

It is suffering, however, which seem to move Goldstein the most, leading him to recall the final days before his wife's death:

my kids
play or cry
in the hospital
compound,
their mother's nearing the end

The questions of sexuality are also personal. Many of the tanka in 'Minimalist Sexuality' reveal the poet's longing for the touch of a loved one:

what good's
self-touching
at night?
give me delirium
through this midnight mind

Tanka in this section describe being alone with one's desires, knowing that years ago he was "wrapped in desire", but now knows that "this celibacy / will last and last".

Nor can Goldstein rely on nature, since in the section Nature, the speaker can only perceive wind, winter, rain, freezing weather, fog and snow:

in the distance
snow ridges
beyond rice-less fields,
I'm Tokyo bound
trying to unwind

The warmth of nature seems out of reach, and such tanka are full of longing which projects itself onto the very landscape.

'Cleanliness, Whiteness, Purity' is more concerned with the question of household duties, such as doing the laundry, dusting, and vacuuming. The poet moves into the coffee shop —his favourite setting in which to write:

no one
bothers me
for tips,
at the rickety table
poems come out minimalist

Death is, of course, more concerned with the question of mortality. Many of the tanka in this section are elegiac, with some moving poems recalling past times: childhood, youth, the death of his wife, the death of family members:

how I cried
when my brother's
first wife died,
every now and then
I cry for my dead wife

Goldstein's double allegiance to America and Japan emerge through the section 'Food, Drink', particularly through the motif of the oriental:

my stomach
swells along
this oriental road,
the bread, the rice,
the chopstick mixture

to the USA cuisine:

donuts
I devour
this long morning
their memory
impossible to appease

In 'Zen, God, Faith, Doubt', the sense of the personal voice rings with an awareness of life's complexities and sadnesses, a world of ambiguities and joy, which is perfectly heard in Goldstein's contemplations in Zen:

the anguish
sits
forever,
oh, this Buddhist
belly

Goldstein's style in 'Minimilast Humor' is spare and often enigmatic and, with tanka such as the first in this section, observant and wry:

the old teacher
along the corridor
picking his nose,
he greets me
with a bow

making cryptic references to the "old teacher" and the delicate bow he makes to his observer. It's not surprising that a man of Goldstein's experience takes huge leaps in compressed moments of rumination. The following tanka, for instance

ho!
there's a gaijin
and another,
this me
I call Japanese

briefly addresses what living in a foreign country means to him.

There's a delightful humor of perception and encounter in 'Minimalist Humor'. What is seen, what is encountered, people and stories: these things may seem nothing to write home about. But Goldstein is, in a way, always writing for himself, and often this is to very considerable effect. To take one example from his lifetime of teaching:

> my voice
> disintegrates
> on "Daisy"—
> the end of back-to back
> classes

The same freshness of perception can also be seen in the following tanka:

> the burp
> at the next
> table,
> how content that Japanese
> with his toothpick

As I think these tanka show, Goldstein has a way of making us aware of the humor of everyday life. Other examples of his distinctive humour I would recommend are "jumping rope" and "my poems".

In two of his tanka in the final section, 'Minimalist Multitudes', "was it / her precious voice" and "how easy /one fills gaps," he achieves the most successful of minimalist tanka and makes them seem effortless. Goldstein's writing is often beautifully relaxed, yet never lax; sometimes pithy, sometimes more expansive, never inflated, nor wordy.

Predominantly, the reader of *This Short Life* is offered fragments, terse five-line poems capturing a thought, an experience, a memory, something seen or heard. Often enigmatic and richly suggestive, these short poems are luminous moments in the poet's long life. They are never boring, but modest in their claims on the reader. They are also highly controlled. The tanka are rhythmically and phonologically neatly shaped poems that sing as well as record.

The front cover of *This Short Life* includes a wonderful portrait of Goldstein by Kazuaki Wakui, which makes the poet, in familiar headgear, putting on his coat, look relaxed and ready to tackle more poems. This alone—lovely as it is—would be worth the price of the book.

# Review: "I Take My Coffee Black"

## Sanford Goldstein's *This Short Life* and the Idea of Minimalist Tanka

### Reviewed by Charles D. Tarlton

*This Short Life : Minimalist Tanka*
Sanford Goldstein
Edited by M. Kei
ISBN-13: 978-1494845599 (Print) 164 pp
$15.00 USD / £ 9.00 GBP / € 11.00 EUR
$5.00 USD (Kindle)

*CARMODY: I have published more than 5,000 tanka
these last few years!*
*BLIGHT: Any of them memorable?*

### I

I probably too readily accepted M. Kei's invitation to review Sanford Goldstein's *This Short Life*. From the blurbs by Michael McClintock, Michael Dylan Welch, and Joy McCall, as well as the "Afterword," written by Kei himself, it was obvious that I was in the presence of a very important tanka poet and that this was something of a pioneering book, a collection of purely "minimalist" tanka, tanka written from a perspective entirely different from my own.

I should be clear. I am more or less a syllable counter when writing tanka, generally staying with the 5/7/5/7/7 syllable count. I realize that things like the number of lines and syllables, as well as all the other desiderata floating around out there for defining "the ideal tanka,"[1] are only arbitrary considerations. I prefer the discipline of syllable counting because it often forces me to discard the first words that might have come to mind and makes me sort through other possible ways of saying things, leading sometimes even to better thing to say. In the final draft, considerations of flow and tempo may require adjusting the strict syllable count, but not the overall shape of the poem. Spontaneity is all right, of course, but it is not itself the guarantee of anything. It could be wonderful, or not.

Goldstein belongs, as it were, to the inspirational school of minimalist tanka, disavowing the interference that comes from too much attention to form. Listen to this from his introduction:

> What happens when we are writing a traditional tanka or one with longer and shorter lines is that the concentration is broken, for we are trying for a 5 or 7 syllable line. The same is true for short-long-short-long-long, a recent adoption which I have liked more than the 31-syllable form. We are always aware that we need syllables or have too many or want to settle for a longer line. So while we are writing a tanka, the concentration is limited, changes appear quite frequently, and sometimes we find we have to start over. In other words, something happened to the original feeling we had.

---

[1] Amelia Fielden, Denis Garrison, and Robert D. Wilson, "A Definition of the ideal form of traditional tanka written in English," Summer, 2009.

I am not a believer in the superiority of first blush, however, as art seldom reaches its goal in the first hit of the hammer, the first paint stroke, or the first flurry of words. Goldstein's argument that the poet's concentration will be broken by having to worry about the requirements of form, rings hollow to me, a distortion of the creative process. The painter, the poet, the composer does not so much start with an immediate beauty, but works toward it stopping when it has been achieved. The process as Goldstein describes it is all but automatic.

A minimalist poem gets its immediacy and we write it down. Often that is the way it is—an image, an event, a memory, a poem with an immediacy that does not require juggling. Of course there are times when we want to change a word or line, but the immediacy is still there.

There is a kind of romanticism that underpins this, the idea that the poem must come directly from the soul or emotions of the poet without mediation, reflect raw insight, emotion, or memory. The poet has the poem, so to speak, as one might have a dream; it comes to him/her and gets written down immediately. This is Goldstein:

Something appears in the mind and before one realizes it, the poem has been formed. Of course it may be revised or rewritten several times but the core of the image remains. And still I think spontaneity is the major clue. That is how I think the process works.

Whether a process like the one described works is not really the question (although I believe Goldstein here has misapprehended it); what matters is whether what comes to the poet immediately as he writes is the best way to say what's on the poet's mind.

The tanka in *This Short Life* are a diarist's record of mostly small observations, feelings, events, ideas, sentiments, reflections, and recollections over the year 2008. Interestingly, in 2007, in his essay, 'This Elusive Tanka World,'[2] Goldstein prepared readers for the kind of thing that stands behind *This Short Life*, when he quoted at length from Takuboku.

Poetry must not be what is usually called poetry. It must be an exact report, an honest diary, of the changes in a man's emotional life. Accordingly, it must be fragmentary; it must not have organization. . . [N]ow I am writing tanka as if I were writing a diary. Perhaps there are well-written diaries and badly written ones, but the value of a diary does not vary according to the writer's skill. A diary is of value only to the writer, and the value is quite irrelevant to the outsider. 'I felt so and so' or 'I thought so and so'—this is all that my tanka purport now. They have no other meaning, none above that.

Goldstein's tanka in *This Short Life* are fragmentary and commonplace in just the way he describes. They are arranged topically around the ideas of "Kids," "Minimalist Sexuality," "Nature," "Death," "Purity," "Death," "Food, Drinks," "Zen," "Humor," and what is called, "Minimalist Multitudes." And most of these tanka really are indeed but fleeting diary jottings in which quick notice is being taken of day-to-day things. The bulk of these tanka make no pretence to Art; they rely on the simplest forms of expression. Because these observations are so simple and employ so few words, they seem out of place to me when they are written out in five lines, like a child wearing an adult's coat. They might have fared better had they actually been kept as simple diary entries.

Consider these very short tanka from the first few pages of *This Short Life* (typical, I would argue, of the majority of Goldstein's very minimalist tanka), each of which I have written out here on a single line.

1) my kid carrying it home, her lopsided heart

[2] *Simply Haiku : A Quarterly Journal of Japanese Short Form Poetry.* Vol. 5 No. 2. Summer, 2007.

2) my kid on stage singing Italian, my lips are parched

3) I'm ready to marry her off, my kid's first baked dish

4) my kid tells me to stay out, she's tonight's cook

5) left without will to penetrate that desired space

6) all these legs and arms and eyes, all searching, all wanting

7) take this hat, wind, at your risk—I press down hard to skull

8) wanting to fold this self, the paper crane should be blue

9) a spring shower over the bridge, a white pair of wings

10) the Chinese tea warms, settles, outside, a quiet snow

Each of these little bursts of words tries to capture a fleeting image and each follows the same formula, employing an opening phrase followed by a slightly ironic riposte. Like almost all the tanka in *This Short Life*, they have first lines of no more than two words, which leaves me with the uncomfortable feeling that minimalist here may simply be a synonym for fewer words. The resulting tanka are unexceptionable, of course, but to me, equally, they are mostly forgettable.

What I mean is this: imagine a writer, someone out of Borges, for example, bent on capturing every detail of life on a single day. It would, of course, be impossible; no one could visualize and express images and events fast enough to keep up with the flow on even the most ordinary day of the most ordinary life. Choices would have to be made and I assume that's what has been going on in Goldstein's "spilling" of tanka. Even so, every short sentence describing something one has seen or felt does not of itself rise to the level of poetry.

These minimalist tanka consist of words to the effect that "this happened, then that; I saw this and I thought that." The question is whether that amounts to poetry. To be really vital, minimalism has to mean something other than just "short." On the positive side, minimalist should designate work that cuts through

unnecessary detail to expose the irreducible core of some human experience, making it sharper, more intense, more powerful. Think of Hemingway, Donald Barthelme, George Oppen, Agnes Martin, and Robert Creeley.

There is a logical and formal difficulty at the doorway to tanka in English. In the beginning, among the Japanese, tanka was subject to many rules and traditions; it was a poetic form as strictly defined as almost any traditional type of English verse. Tone, subject matter, number of "syllables" (31), number of "sections or parts" (5), pivots, and so on. Tanka in Japanese tends to adhere to rules about these things, especially those dealing with the form or structure (although there has been more flexibility in Japanese regarding the number of "lines" than in anything else).

But, in English tanka there is far more confusion and disagreement. The only certain specification, when all is said and done, has been the five lines. But, if we can do away with line length, with rhythms and syllabic meter, with appropriate subject matter, with tone and color, and so forth, why can't we abandon the rule of five lines? We can, of course, and there are many instances of three- and four-line tanka in English, but the innovations have yet to take hold. Because, if the last bastion of five lines is lost, all we would have is the idea of a short free-verse poem. All that we believe to be distinctive about tanka in English would be out the door.

I think a further and more important answer lies in the need for some sort of discipline in the creative process. When you have reduced the idea of a tanka to an eleven-syllable expression, like this by Goldstein;

my kid
tells me
to stay out,
she's tonight's
cook

the insistence on five lines is a little groundless. We might write it out in three lines just as appropriately.

my kid tells me
to stay out
she's tonight's cook

Suppose we were just to write it out like the Japanese once did, in a single line, a monostich? Then we would get this:

my kid tells me to stay out, she's tonight's cook

What happens here, of course, is that this "tanka" fades away, I think, and is exposed for the everyday reportage that it is. Any remaining poetic patina derives solely from the odd phrasing, the placement of the comma, in particular. There is no depth of meaning, no ambiguity, and no metaphorical extension. If we rewrite this with a more ordinary syntax, then we get something like the following;

My kid tells me to stay out of the kitchen.
She is cooking tonight.

Now unless we are willing to place the major emphasis in tanka poetry on brevity for its own sake, requiring the reader to supply whatever directions of meaning might hide behind the barebones phrasing, we have to be prepared to allow that more words may often make for greater and subtler communication and that minimalism is not, in itself, a virtue.

So, the next question must be whether there is some kind of minimum length for a poem proper, especially a tanka? Seriously, if Goldstein's eleven syllables are enough to constitute a tanka, then how about eight or fewer? Consider this concocted example:

worlds
glimpsed
on each
side
of the glass

This might easily be mistaken as a fragment from e. e. cummings or even a loose translation of something from Sappho, but I do not see how

can it be a tanka—except that five lines has become the sole determining criterion.

But, rather than enter any farther into this quagmire of what is and what isn't a tanka, can we just say that the five lines, written as one,

worlds glimpsed on each side of the glass

is really only a fragment, at best an epigram or an aphorism? If the argument remains inconclusive and, yet, no other rule than that of five lines is forthcoming, then what about this?

each
word
hurts
that much
more

The words *poet* and *poetry* derive, of course, from the Greek *poiesis*, which does not mean to catch or spill but to make. Poetry may spring from inspiration, but the poet is someone who sculpts and shapes that raw product of inspiration, not necessarily to preserve the poet's first verbalization, but to present the poetic glimpse in ways that allow the reader to experience and feel something like what the poet felt and understood.

II

*". . . poetry,—the best words in their best order."*
—*Coleridge*

In my judgment, *This Short Life* (as is often the case in books of tanka) is too long and contains too many poems. Long collections (163 pages, 356 tanka, in this case) of short poems inevitably include a lot of work that might better have stayed behind in the notebooks. That being said, however, I would like in this second section to turn to several of Goldstein's best tanka, ones that seem to me to rise above the rest in *This Short Life*, and explore them more closely. In amongst the many brief and perfunctory tanka in *This Short Life* there are many that, to my mind, fully attain the status of poetry. Here are a few tanka representative of those best.

> how silent
> that corner of flesh,
> that hidden space,
> I should have had
> a pair of ragged claws

First of all, we might ask just what this poem is talking about; the Editor has put it in the section entitled "Minimalist Sexuality," but I have trouble making that kind of sense of it. "[T]hat corner of flesh, / that hidden space" seems anything but sexual to me, at least not in any romantic or lustful sense. The "pair of ragged claws" seems particularly inappropriate in that connection.

So, starting from the first lines— "how silent / that corner of flesh / that hidden space," I read this as relating to the poet's frustration in the face of death, his wife's death and her disease locked up, silent, in the hidden space of her brain, and to the poet wishing for the means of clawing the disease out—" I should have had / a pair of ragged claws." The poem is powerful, a little enigmatic, and very musical as well; just listen to the near sprung rhymes of "flesh" and "space" and "had," "pair," and "claws." The syllabic beat within the lines is generous as well— 3/5/4/4/6.

> I leap
> into my brother's mind
> across continents,
> I pour the Pacific
> into a vase of sad flowers

This is a beautiful tanka in my opinion, deep in its meanings, mysterious, rhythmically balanced on the pivot of "across continents," and powerful at the end. How could you improve on that "I leap / into my brother's mind?" And how many things does he say at once with that pouring "the Pacific / into a vase of sad flowers?" I have no idea what this poem is precisely about, but I have heard the voice of my own brother calling across the continent to tell me of our father's death and I am sure that falls within the compass of Goldstein's verse.

> how bright
> tonight's light
> in the falling snow,
> I raise bright images
> to calm my desperate hands

You could actually sing this tanka! And, again, the pivot, "in the falling snow," is virtually perfect, balancing "tonight's bright light" over against the "bright images" of his poems that calm the poet's "desperate hands." The light (is it moonlight, street lights, the windows of distant houses?) is mirrored in the writing by which the poet seeks to quiet his trembling (desperate hands). And, again, it is more than just a flash of perception; Goldstein uses more fully developed lines here (2/3/5/6/7), minimalist only in the first two. In fact, the way it is written belies even the mere five lines; there are four phases or stages here.

> how bright
> tonight's light
>
> tonight's light
> in the falling snow,
>
> in the falling snow
> I raise bright images
>
> I raise bright images
> to calm my desperate hands

The message is complex, reverberating, and very poetic.

> up the steep
> slope
> where once we ran,
> the long decades up
> and down

This is another very musical tanka, and a very good use of variable line length. The "slope" seems all the steeper for slipping down so abruptly, and, after another delightful pivot, a similar device works in the second part.

> the long decades up
> and down

Top to bottom, we might say, or all over the place. The characterization of life as a slope "where once we ran / the long decades" is a very successful metaphor that extends easily out to the last line.

> the page fills
> with red scrawls
> of poetry,
> they crowd into
> commonplace corners

The central image that takes up the first half of this tanka is alive, literally. Those "red scrawls" are like bits of flesh or words written in blood, poetry that fills up the page, crowding into the corners in the second part. There is a lot to say here and it is said succinctly, deliberately and well. Goldstein's image is that of a passionate poetry whose flow can barely be contained.

There is a tension here between the poet's "red" feelings, his manic scrawling, and the notion of the "commonplace corners." The poem might even be said to enact the larger tensions in *This Short Life* between the poet's resolution to create minimalist tanka and the *gravitas* that so often floods his thought. He wants to write little tanka about the mundane details of life, but he keeps running up against larger issues that are determined to find their way into richer tanka.

> her voice
> like fragile
> threads,
> the bright needle
> in her hand

Much of the force of this tanka derives from exactly not being routine or workaday. The "needle" and the "fragile threads" at first suggest some kind of sewing, perhaps even weaving, but there is not enough information to know exactly what. Then we notice that it is not threads at all he is talking about, but a female voice that is "like fragile threads." But then what is the "needle in her hand?" Is it a real needle we are supposed to imagine, a sewing needle, or another kind, are we watching a singing seamstress or hearing the soft cries of a patient in a hospital? Take out the comma and we get a poignant single sentence: "her voice threads the bright needle in her hand" and the image now is even more magical. So he made it into a poem.

Here is the final example of what I would say is truly a minimalist tanka.

> no wax
> on those temple floors,
> only the daily rub-down,
> a rub-down
> with damp cloths

This tanka is short (2/5/6/3/3) and everyday, but is still able to transport the reader to exotic places, where the everyday is timeless. We can virtually hear the hush or imagine subtle chiming somewhere in an old temple, the floors smooth and worn from endless "rub-downs," not with wax or polish, but simple "damp cloths." I can almost smell the floor as it slowly dries, catch glimpses of pensive monks in the shadows, and I feel an involuntary piety that makes me want to bow my head just a little. This poem takes a simple observation and creates a world out of it, and I think that if minimalism is to mean anything in tanka poetry this must be the standard by which we judge efforts in that direction. Short lines and commonplace reports will not be enough.

# Review: *circling smoke, scattered bones* by Joy McCall

## Reviewed by Brian Zimmer

*circling smoke, scatters bones*
by Joy McCall
Keibooks, Perryville, Maryland, USA, 2013
$US 15.00 ppb / $US 5.00 Kindle
ISBN: 978-0615880006

When M. Kei asked me to review Joy McCall's book of tanka, *Circling Smoke, Scattered Bones,* I felt waves of immense privilege rush over me. In the manner of waves, another that felt something like panic immediately followed the first. It was the realization of the overwhelming nature of the task I had agreed to. These two waves continue dashing over me, and I have a slightly discomfiting sense that the tide may be flowing in. Were it ebbing, I might justifiably expect to find the necessary remains of driftwood, shells, old bones, perhaps a bottled message or two left on the shore. I might possibly find the essential objects necessary for a sensible review of McCall's extraordinary book.

The fact that *circling smoke, scattered bones* is something of an *oeuvre* more properly calls for an overview than a review, something lengthier than the good editor of *Atlas Poetica* could expect. Why is it I have the sneaking suspicion he is leaning back in his chair, feet up on his desk, having a good laugh at my expense? You see, he is partly to blame for my dilemma. It was he who took the hundreds (yes, hundreds) of tanka McCall sent him and masterfully shaped and stitched them into the impossibly intricate quilt that is this collection.

So let me attempt the impossible, admitting with apologies that I will not—I cannot—do *circling smoke, scattered bones*, or its author, justice.

Like Takuboku and Saito before her, Joy McCall is an intensely candid, autobiographical poet. To be trite: "You couldn't make this stuff up." She pulls no punches from the first page to the last.

after the crash
left me paralysed
forever—
a fortune cookie:
'you will always be safe'

A motorcycle accident a decade ago left McCall paraplegic, living and writing from her wheelchair in the ancient English town of Norwich, England. Like her fifteenth-century townswoman, the great mystic Julian of Norwich —who, by her own will, lived-out her life imprisoned in a hermitage with a single window and a cat—Joy McCall still "gets around." Like Julian from her hermitage, McCall is also a visionary. From her wheelchair, she soars over the British landscape with its earthen mounds, ruined castles, and waterways that empty into the sea.

my skin
glows blue and silver
the dark room fills
with the sound of wings and waves
the flying fish are calling

McCall quite literally gets around, her rolling carriage gives her a permanent seat at the local pub, once part of an old monastery. Like much of Norwich, it seems, the monastery-pub is haunted.

in the old hall
where the strangers dwelt
a robed rabbi walks
he repeats the sacred words
there is no flesh on his white bones

A rabbi? Such ghostly anomalies are apparently taken for granted in Norwich. At the very least, by Joy McCall. Norwich boasts the most churches in England, along with the most unbelievers and witches. Here are the ancient paths where the island's Aboriginal people, Romans, and Vikings, intersect. Of course McCall, with something of the Druid and witch about her, is always on the side of early Britain's own Joan of Arc, Boudicca, and all painted warriors. No matter who wins the war, it is always the most daring, vulnerable, proud, and tenacious who are the real victors in McCall's world.

my fingers
stroking the new tattoo
on my old stump
wanting the snake to wake
uncoil and fill the space

the king's men
turned to pitted stone
by old witches
I long to dance again
in that small grey circle

Today family and friends drive her out to her beloved countryside where she was once known to park her motorcycle and spend her nights in stone circles, naming the stars in five lines.

Did I mention that Norwich also has one of the highest crime rates in the country? Many of the "crooks," as she affectionately calls them, know Joy McCall by name. They visit her, help with what wants doing about the house and garden, and bring their illegitimate newborns for her blessing. No matter that some of them are only sixteen years old. That seems to be something of a median age for first fathers in Norwich.

on remand
he comes to say goodbye
once again
the tidal pattern
of this friendship

father and son
banned from meeting
by the courts
sit in the tent of the willow
arm in arm, weeping

Family, friends, saints, and sinners people Joy McCall's world. And children. They trust her with their confidences, their fears and sorrows. McCall is never condescending or even maternal with them. She is the one thing all children look for in a grown-up: an older, trustworthy friend who really listens, looks them in the eye, and takes them seriously. One gets the feeling McCall prefers the company of this motley gathering of the innocent, law-breaking, hurting, and wise (often all four attributes in a single boy), to that of most adults.

the boy
is of two parts: playing
then thinking
he says all things
like coins, have two sides

in the great court
before the bewigged judge
the boy stands
he swears to tell the truth
he lies, saving his father from jail

I ask the boy,
"how are you so wise
so young?"
he says, "disappointments,"
and shrugs, and smiles

So many poems haunt the reader in this collection. Ghosts, both real and imaginative (McCall makes no distinction), crises of faith, madwomen, mothers, daughters, magic wands, spells, candles, prayer—all are sung with near-perfect pitch in the beautiful amplitude that is this book.

Few are the tanka collections I would call "page-turners." This is one of them. Whereas most tanka collections open quietly like heavy blooms inviting the reader to take her or his time to savor and contemplate their perfume, *Circling Smoke, Scattered Bones* only permits the reader a quick promise to him or herself to "get back to this one . . . and this one . . . this section . . . let me bookmark this page . . . ." It is a map ineluctably unrolling at the pace of life as lived. A map so detailed and rich, covering so much territory between its covers, one wants to rest but is compelled to keep reading even when tears of laughter or despair blind one's eyes. If McCall weren't confined to it herself, we might be tempted to beg for her wheelchair just to sit down and keep up with her pace. ("Aww, come on, you know it's funny," I can hear her say to those who may have just gasped.)

It is no exaggeration to acknowledge that I have never seen the likes of such a book of tanka in my many years as reader and poet. Quite honestly, it is one of the best books of tanka—no, one of the best books of poems I have ever read. I know from other online voices that I am not alone in heralding these poems. "This book! I'm crying! It's amazing!"

Is the book perfect? To many it will seem slightly flawed from a "technical" standpoint where normative English tanka is concerned. Does it matter? I don't think so. The reader barely has time to analyze individual tanka the turning of pages accelerating in anticipation of what comes next. Does it matter to McCall? When getting too cerebral discussing poetics, tanka history, etc., with her, she simply shrugs, confessing, "Oh, I'm sure you're right. I don't know anything about that stuff. I've been writing for fifty years and simply fell in love with the tanka form. I can't help it. I now THINK in five-lines. You know I'm really just a peasant. You only think my poems are good because you happen to like them."

I do like them. Unfortunately I can't give them their due in a simple review. I can only try to whet your appetite and urge you to acquire the book. If you do, be prepared for a long night ahead, one that will feel like minutes. McCall is an original. If nothing else, read her to discover the 'something else' in a voice you have never heard before in English tanka.

Yes, I like them very much. I'm not alone. I'm pretty sure you will like them too, finding this uniquely narrative book of extended tanka sequences and strings—spellbinding.

in the circle
on the windy hill
a small box
inside, a tied scroll
with the words "there is no end"

Brian Zimmer
January, 2014

# One for Sorrow : Joy McCall's Tanka for Weathering the Storm

## Reviewed by Charles D. Tarlton

circling smoke, scattered bones
by Joy McCall
Keibooks, Perryville, Maryland, USA, 2013
$US 15.00 ppb / $US 5.00 Kindle
ISBN: 978-0615880006

Writing is the supreme solace.
—W. Somerset Maugham

1

The tanka poems in Joy McCall's circling smoke, scattered bones cover a great many subjects — trees, flowers, birds, talk, longing, the fields, strangers, relatives, children, the young, widows, neighbors, families, the seashore, plants, the seasons, weather, the countryside, ruins, ghosts, churches, pubs, prisoners, old age, death, dreams, spiders, pain, treatment, doctors, cafes, loss, witchcraft, religion, snakes, Christmas, and husbands. The poems are beautiful, well-crafted, sensitive, generous, and imaginative.

Let me show you what I mean; here are four of her tanka, chosen pretty much at random:

sepia photo
of some brown sheep resting
in an old barn
cracked beams, straw, and hens
pecking in the dirt—that's all

what would I put
in the open mouth
of the snake?
words, small poems, coiling
in circles to the tail

on the cliff edge
walks an old woman, talking
to herself
through her grey body
I see the waves breaking

now I have been
in dreams to your bay
where the great ships sail
I hear that same voice
of the sea, calling

From this sampling we notice that McCall's tanka are regular, at least in line length, always (or most often) S/L/S/L/L. But, they are also very musical and rhythmical in their unfolding. Listen to this again:

sepia photo
of some brown sheep resting

or this

what would I put
in the open mouth
of the snake?

We are in the presence of a natural singer, a poet's voice for sure. Line after line, the music drives our reading. Go back, and listen to that third tanka again.

on the cliff edge
walks an old woman, talking
to herself

God, I can hear the likeness to

*As cool as the pale wet leaves
of lily-of-the-valley*

That's Ezra Pound, of course. Here's some more of the same from McCall.

through her grey body
I see the waves breaking

Sounds like Pound again. Or is it Stevens, or Yeats?

It is in poems like these that McCall moves among the people, places and goings-on in her English world. She pokes her poet's nose in everywhere and takes away images and ideas with which to fashion her poems. And, if this were all there was to this book, it would still be worth our while to read and study. Joy McCall has a lot to teach us about the craft of tanka poetry and about the poetic soul that goes far beyond mere skill at words.

But there is a further dimension to *circling smoke, scattered bones* that lifts it out of the bin of just good or even very good poetry, something that marks it with a kind of importance that we do not often see. Sorrow is woven through the text of *circling smoke, scattered bones*, to create a vibrant and variegated fabric, but one with dark backgrounds. Not every poem confronts pain and loss, but enough of them do to prevent us from thinking of these poems as 'adventures in Norfolk' or 'country walks.' McCall's sorrow is not simple, though, not a recitation of sad and painful things, and let it go at that, but a sorrow that comes with a twist, a flash of wit, irony, or empathy that lets the reader see over it, so to speak.

Most of the tanka in the book generally have a symmetrical formal organization. The opening lines set the action by stating a general principle, recording a feeling, making an observation, and the like. Usually, this takes up the first three lines, but as often the third line is also a separate pivot or a line that fits syntactically into both the opening and the finish. Here is a randomly chosen and beautiful example of one of her openings:

no cuckoo calls
over the hill where we sit
listening

The resolution will come in the last two lines, which most of the time swerve slightly and carry the poetic impact, lifting the whole ensemble to its intended, dramatic, and redemptive height. Her endings are not just the faux-Zen endings that so often conclude tanka in English; they are like a combination punch in boxing, a left hook followed by a right uppercut. That "listening" in the third line above creates just the slightest pause, and then the poem finishes this way:

but suddenly, skylarks
singing high above the ruins

You have to love that "suddenly, skylarks."

But, I don't think anyone coming to these poems will quickly or casually get beyond the first chapter, *after the crash*, which explores the event and aftermath of a motorcycle accident in which McCall lost a leg and which, as she puts it, *left me paralyzed/forever*. This mishap, and the strategy she has developed for dealing with it, underpins the art of her poetry of *sorrow* and provides means for coping with sorrow that emerge first from the accident and then ramify across life (and the book) as a whole. Most of the poems in Joy McCall's tanka collection, *circling smoke, scattered bones*, are saturated with the effort to overcome sorrow. The vehicle for such transcendence is the act of poetry itself, the making of tanka.

Her sorrow, as a concept (and maybe even in the actual experience) contains, in a dialectical way, the idea of solace. I don't mean that the poet buries her head in words and pretends things are not as bad as they really are, but that she drags the pain of her life (the details of real suffering and loss) up into her poems and then transfigures that pain in the dynamic of her thoughts and words. I believe that is the pattern in which the poems themselves are composed and the strategy by which she seeks to encompass her own sorrow.

The motorbike wreck and its aftermath colors most of what is talked about in this first section—the pain, the weeping, the loss, the longing for what had been. And then there is this wonderful tanka summing up everything.

sorrow falls
a heavy dead weight
I want to go
where my feet can't take me
where love lies sleeping

The epicenter of *circling smoke, scattered bones* lies in the intersection of, first, McCall's motorcycle accident and its aftermath, and, then, her attempt, poetically, to express, encompass, and thereby counterpoise the symbols of that suffering. Now, of course, such overcoming is not easily possible in the natural world, but poetry does not do its work there anyway. In the way the poems work, the carefully chosen symbols, images, and descriptions of *sorrow* are trumped by other words. Here is a major example. The first half or opening:

after the crash
left me paralysed
forever —

"Forever" makes you want to take a little breath here, create an expectation, and then comes this:

a fortune cookie:
'you will always be safe'

The first three lines, the set-up, state the elements of horror—*paralysed* and *forever*. As we feel the full force of this jarring frankness, she turns away, as it were, and finds solace in the fantasy in a fortune cookie—'*you will always be safe.*'

Now, such symbolic action changes nothing in the physical world of real illness and injury. But, it does work in that allusive dimension where attitudes, however, can change. Injury exists, as it were, on one dimension or plane, the physical, but sorrow exists on another, the spiritual, one might say, or the imaginative. Sorrow is an attitude toward things, something painful, unpleasant, or sad, to be sure, but as attitude, it implies a gesture, this way or that, and how.[1] So here we find McCall delving deeply into irony for a point of view in which her tragedy can be momentarily transcended. Here is how it works:

> we write
> of body parts
> detached
> my leg, his hand: trying
> to hold ourselves together

In another tanka in this opening series McCall pursues solace by similar but even more fiercely ironic methods, an "it-could-have-been-worse" strategy.

> bone-bits and gravel
> work their way to the surface
> after all these years
> the road still reminds me
> how nearly it took my life

And the same maneuver is on display in still another motorcycle tanka; if anything, this poem is even more ironic but similarly comforting.

> how is it
> that I miss the old bike
> more than my feet?
> the sound of an engine
> brings instant tears

The poem as magic, spell, or incantation is at work in all the dimensions these poems seek to inhabit. Here is one last bike-crash poem (one that actually appears later on) before we turn to the wider manifestations of sorrow in the rest of the book.

> Irish whiskey
> the best dampener
> for this pain
> four-leaf clover growing
> out of a crack in the wall

This poem realizes everything I have been saying about McCall's take on sorrow; what could be more evocative of the magic spell than the idea of a "dampener" for pain? And here there are two of them—Irish whiskey (maybe even a practical, if short-term, balm) and the four-leaf clover (pure magic).

2

In this second section, I want to range rather freely over the whole of McCall's text, pausing here and there to sample the flavor of her playful poetic therapy. Well, actually more than that. Because there are so many poems in the book (mostly five to the page for 170 pages or so) I worry that they might not all receive the close attention they deserve. So, I am limiting myself to examination of just a few poems, but I will be looking at them close up and asking questions about how they work. I want to encourage readers to examine the working of the rest of these poems.

Early in *circling smoke, scattered bones*, we encounter two poems that powerfully enact the overcoming of sorrow. The first is this:

> young thin waitress
> *only the strong survive*
> tattooed on her chest
> the italic words shielding
> her heart's fragility

The world of sorrow (here represented by a "heart's fragility") is checked by an assertive tattoo on a young woman's chest that stands in direct opposition, *"only the strong survive."* Of course we know the tattooed message is largely bravado, but it is nonetheless designed to insulate the fragility, a sort of overcompensation that is all too familiar. At first, I thought that the message being in italics was meant to signify the poet's quoting something, as it were, from the text of the woman's chest, but as the poem eventually

---

[1] I. A. Richards, *Principles of Literary Criticism* (1925), xv. 112. "These imaginal and incipient activities or tendencies to action, I shall call attitudes."

discloses, the tattoo was itself written in italics. But, why call attention twice to this detail in five lines? I think because McCall wanted us to see the tattoo mainly as a statement and a prophylactic measure, symbolic or verbal action meant to provide the solace of hope or a dream to neutralize suffering in advance.

In the very next poem on the page, the strategy is even more beautifully illustrated. In the first movement of the poem we get the elements of genuine sorrow,

> a widow now
> she sells her house
> to travel the world

But before we are drawn wholly into the malaise of death, the loss of home, and a pathetic escapism, we are spun around, and given a sardonic second look:

> even death in a far country
> is better than the void

In a world of tragic stories, even death takes on a quasi-positive hue and extricates the widow and the reader from despair.

After several poems variously close to or far away from the underlying scheme, in which sorrow is laid bare only to be veiled in irony, we come to another pair of poems that not only enact the strategy but express it literally. In the first, the wind pulls the viewer back from an abandoned and sea-worn oar (tossed up in the swash, I am imagining):

> I cannot look
> at the old worn oak oar
> where it lies

But, the pathos of that image is not allowed to prevail and we immediately get this:

> the wind, blustering
> calls me to the sea again

In the very next poem the rhythms of the sea reverse position and, now coming first, they

explicitly serve to cast the poet's sorrow literally to the wind.

> a low voice
> carried on the wind
> on the tides
> pulls my sorrow
> over the hills and far away

The section called "yellow chrysanthemums" reminds me of another tanka pairing earlier on. Here are the two poems playing their separate riffs on reds (or pink) and yellow.

> no lady
> would wear pink and yellow
> together
> the wild geranium patch
> sprinkled with buttercups

> the red-faced goldfinch
> is picking yellow petals
> from dandelions
> to line his nest with the soft
> golden fragrance of flowers

In both of these cases, the worlds of humans and of nature are at first distinguished and then brought together; the "wild geranium patch/ sprinkled with buttercups" refutes the proper lady's refusal ever to wear "pink with yellow" and the instinctive gesture of the goldfinch in picking out dandelion petals to line his nest yields him "the golden fragrance of flowers," a purely human conception.

The motif of sorrow returns before long, again with the petals of flowers, but this time squarely in the demesne of dying and the dead.

> the wake over,
> the chrysanthemum petals
> have all fallen

By now we are waiting for the image to swing around again, away from death and more in the direction of regeneration. The word "fallen" is transformed into an act of creation, and the poem concludes:

on bare stems, thin new roots,
golden blooms will come again

Anyone who has had a loved one committed to an old folks home or, more euphemistically, 'an assisted living facility,' will know the surreal dimensions of such places. At-one-time-real persons now wander in drug-induced stupors muttering incomprehensibles. Any resident with any sensibility remaining is constantly on the lookout for avenues of escape. Something not unlike this bitter sentiment sits behind McCall's much calmer and less critical words:

day is done
old people go to their beds
at the Home

But she has allowed an anonymous "she" to do the talking:

she waits in her Sunday best
for a ride to church

As I jump around in this book in the search for songs of sorrow, I can't help but notice that not all of these poems are optimistic. In many cases the effort to twist images into dreams, into wishes that might come true, is just too hard. But still the music has a sort of power of its own, and the turn in the middle of the tanka betrays the tendency, if nothing else, and shows us McCall leaning into hope in the face of sorrow.

A good example of a strategy abandoned or just not working comes from a tanka in the section called *over the hills and far away*. The opening leads straight to the sorrow:

I wept
I want my youth back
and he sang me

And after the bridge the singing avails little or nothing:

a song of rivers,
of loss, and passing time

Lines from the old nursery rhyme about the consequences of coming upon magpies, what happens whether you spy one or two or more, are ripped from their childish context and we get a more bitter and warlike image:

the long-tailed magpies
in all their cruel beauty
are gathering now,
bickering, fighting, mating

A bit of the old rhyme is salvaged, but it leads only to her mocking conclusion: 'one for sorrow, two for joy.' A little later on, however, the magpies return in a slightly altered conceit, sidestepping the pessimism, but only at the last minute.

two magpies
on the broken chimney
in the sunshine
sometimes, despair is deep
but it's 'two for joy'

In another poem, the theme of sorrow and its terministic banishment returns with a vengeance. There is evidence here of a psychology of sorrow. McCall moves effortlessly and gracefully from a very poetic depiction of a moment in pure nature (tinged, albeit, with metaphor),

on dark chestnut leaves
cabbage-white butterflies
wings catching the sun

How gorgeous is that?!

to a more-or-less express statement of the theory of sorrow's banishment in dreams (or poems),

my fragile, flitting dreams
bright against the sadness

The ways her magic works are not always so spiritual, however; often sorrow is banished in very direct and understandable tropes, a redirection of attention, perhaps, or invocations of out of the ordinary agents. Here's one calling upon birds and the wind:

> everything moves
> except the pain
> I ask the gulls
> to carry it to the sea
> the wind to take it away

and another one that depends on the most practical distraction;

> the postman brings
> two books from a distant friend
> I begin to read
> and forget the pain
> and the things I have lost

one that calls for the tactic of just not worrying;

> this year for Lent
> we will give up worrying
> and fretting, and trust
> that life will be forgiving
> when we are frail and careless

and a last one here that calls for an uncanny experience, the kind of experience that makes you shake your head.

> in a night dream
> we danced on the winter lawn
> to a distant flute
> next day I saw wide circles
> in the snow, wet shoes by the door

So, in conclusion, there are many dozens more fabulous tanka in this collection that I have not even mentioned. As I look back over *circling smoke, scattered bones* I know that I have barely scratched the surface of Joy McCall's discernment as a poet. There are too many poems here for any but the bravest and most indefatigable reader to digest properly, but I have beaten that horse enough already. Let me conclude this discussion by bringing in two last poems that 1) reiterate the theme that I think underpins the tanka in *circling smoke, scattered bones*

and 2) at the same time reveal a little more about the poetic craft operating in this book.

In the first we easily imagine the poet as she has over and over described herself. She is ill, as we know, paralyzed from a motorcycle accident, and not getting any better. So, here she is describing a moment in her day:

> I lie down
> briefly to ease the pain

But she is not given to despair, as we know, particularly not in her poetry. Her mind looks to the sky and we sense that the poet is going to dance away from her sorrow on the wings of her poem:

> and the sun breaks
> onto my face, and I know
> the flipside of sadness

This is symbolic escape, accomplished by the poet's faith in the magic of poetic words (even if only a fleeting faith).

Finally, lest we imagine that McCall is completely taken in by her own sorcery, we catch this glimpse of her, in a moment of commonsensical clarity, admitting to a poetic wavering.

> my well-being
> swings on a fragile thread
> caught by the wind
> I'm tossing the coin
> for holding on, letting go

Charles D. Tarlton
San Francisco, California

# ANNOUNCEMENTS

*Atlas Poetica will publish short announcements in any language up to 300 words in length on a space available basis. Announcements may be edited for brevity, clarity, grammar, or any other reason. Send announcements in the body of an email to: AtlasPoetica@gmail.com—do not send attachments.*

## 2014 TSA International Tanka Contest Results

The Tanka Society of America is pleased to announce the winners of the 15th TSA International Tanka Contest, judged by Susan Constable and Michele L. Harvey. A record number of entries were received from poets around the world. The full report including the judges' comments will be published in the Fall issue of *Ribbons* (the TSA journal) as well as on the TSA website.

First Place—Lesley Anne Swanson (USA)

perforations
along this notebook page
almost invisible
the tiny separations
that ease the final parting

Second Place—Jenny Ward Angyal (USA)

on pilgrimage
to Yeats' rag & bone shop—

I hammer
steely scraps of song,
build a monument to loss

Third Place—David Terelinck (Australia)

banking the embers
after the last guest
has departed . . .
this Pandora's box
of deepening silence

Honorable Mentions (not ranked)

Tracy Davidson (UK)

long drought
our prayers for rain
go unanswered
the one cloud on the horizon
mushroom-shaped and growing

Ken Slaughter (USA)

gentle waves
rocking the boats . . .
another storm
my mind predicted
never happens

Christine L. Villa (USA)

only remembering
how he loved me . . .
in a clear brook
white clouds gather
in my hands


Celia Stuart-Powles (USA)

listening
as her memory
slips
the family ghosts
out of the closet

*   *   *

# Mandy's Pages Announces Tanka Contest Winners 2014

Source: http://www.mandys-pages.com/
contests/annual-tanka-contest/170-atc-2014-
results

## The First Place

his false teeth
and her round spectacles
on the side table . . .
do one and one
always add up to two?

Lily Waters - Switzerland


## Second Place

I put sachets of sugar
one after another
in my coffee
his words
are bitter

Radka Mindova - Bulgaria

The Third Place is a tie:

mini umbrella
how much space for love
in the rains
his right shoulder
still drenching

Ajaya Mahala - India


across the room
I stole a look
into your eyes
a thousand veils lifted
at dawn

Asni Amin - Singapore
Readers' Choice Award on Facebook goes to:

snowy egrets
gliding on a carpet
of blue air
breathlessly you tell me
you've fallen out of love

Pamela A. Babusci - USA


*   *   *

# Keibooks Announces
## *Hedgerows, Tanka Pentaptychs,*
## by Joy McCall

Joy McCall takes a keen interest in everything from her children to the local crooks and drunks, artisans, madwomen, and ghosts. The supernatural is as real to her as the material world and the dead populate her poems along with the living. The fleshless rabbi walking his haunted corridor reminds her that Norwich was the origin of the Blood Libel against the Jews, while not far away the witches still dance among the standing stones. Old churches, old pubs, and old graves tell stories to those that listen amid the scattered needles and barroom fights of the present day.

From *Hedgerows*:

I throw
blood-red berries
on the fire
a dark hawthorn spike
pins my soul to the earth

all those
dark ancient spirits
stalk these streets
hiding inside the faces
of passersby

the machines
throw off engine oil
and cutting swarf
exhaustion and despair
dirt and disease

the horse
watches me as I go
and beside him
a woman with red hair
and wild tattoos, laughs

Praise for *Hedgerows:*

"Many was the time, while reading 'hedgerows,' that I sat back in my chair and said 'Wow.' All of the poems in this book are beautiful, many are very moving; a few defy criticism. I believe that Joy McCall's poetic voice is one of the truest and strongest you will ever hear."—Jonathan Day, artist and maker of books

"Joy McCall's voice grows more powerful with her latest collection of tanka, *Hedgerows*. As with her previous book, (*circling smoke, scattered bones*', 'hedgerows' presents tanka of an exceedingly narrative intimacy. Here are poems about the harrowing ordeals of living with disability and its ongoing health crises, poems of deep love and grief often informed by an equally deep ambivalence, poems of profound empathy with landscape and locale, poems of faith, doubt and even the "supernatural." Refusing false demarcations between any aspect of her life, McCall never consents to separate or address them singly.

In the language of Traditional Witchcraft, 'riding the hedge' is an expression for the ecstatic experience of the witch straddling the boundaries between this and the 'Otherworld.' Doing so, s/ he gathers power to affect change in both. For McCall, the hedge she rides takes the form of the pentaptych, a technical form with which she achieves a mastery so unobtrusive, the uninitiated reader might not notice it at all. 'hedgerows' insists on being a book of excellent poetry first, a book of tanka second. Somehow that feels right if slightly daunting to those of us also writing in the genre. At the very least it is the mark of authentic experience, again bringing to our attention a poet of real stature working at the apex of her art."— Brian Zimmer, tanka poet

"*Hedgerows* are part of England's heritage, as fundamental to our landscape as Shakespeare is to our literature. In 1882, William Cobbett in his Rural Rides, described hedgerows 'full of shepherd's rose, honeysuckle and all sorts of wildflowers'; he spoke of walking field to field, with such blooms one side, corn the other: 'pleasure grounds indeed!' Hedgerows are vibrant ecosystems, havens to wildlife, if only we will let them be. Joy McCall understands them . . . and she hears the poetry within.

"These ninety-five tanka pentaptychs (short sequences of five tanka) recall the recently reclaimed art of hedge-laying and bring new stems, or 'pleachers', to tanka's ancient roots. Out of the twisted, tangled darkness come women, witches, ghosts, intensive care units, public houses, graveyards, people and places near and far. Joy's is a life of many lives. She dwells in the belly of the deer. The hymn in her blood 'flows dark back to the soil from whence it came'. She is leaves, berries, hips and haws. Spiders come to weave webs in her hair. She makes deals with the devil.

"Look deep and you, too, will be 'caught in the pentaptych hedgerows', and like their creator, you'll be unlikely 'to come out again anytime soon.'"

—Claire Everett, Editor of *Skylark* & Tanka Prose Editor at *Haibun Today*.

*Hedgerows, Tanka Pentaptychs*
by Joy McCall
Edited by M. Kei
ISBN 978-0692200988 (Print) 176 pp
$13.00 USD (print) or $5.00 USD (Kindle)

Purchase in print at: https://www.createspace.com/4757189

\* \* \*

# Keibooks Announces
## *This Short Life : Minimalist Tanka*
## by Sanford Goldstein

"Sanford thought that *Journeys Far and Near : tanka roads*—his recent collection—would be his last published book. He didn't count on M. Kei being wise enough to know there were far more tanka to be published. I'm guessing, and hoping, that even this present book will not be his last; the old man still has so much to say. He can still write tanka like no one else. Tanka that seem simple but hold deep truths. Tanka that seem complex but go straight to the heart of things. Sanford writes honest, modest poems, that tell the stories of his daily life, following the example of his own hero, Takuboku."—Joy McCall, author of *circling smoke, scattered bones*

Sanford Goldstein, the grand old man of tanka, is now eighty-eight years old. A co-translator of modern classics of Japanese tanka, editor of journals and anthologies, and a gifted poet in the mold of Ishikawa Takuboku, Goldstein has been on his tanka road for fifty years. In his latest book, he says, "[M]inimalism is a state of mind. Something appears in the mind and before one realizes it, the poem has been formed." All the tanka in *This Short Life* have this immediacy. They are uncensored, fresh, honest, and engaged. Rationalization and literary artifice are excluded. They are life as it happens.

the cat
like something
out of Noh,
so delicate its footsteps
in an autumn field

during
the seven-mile
walk,
the dead came along
this April day

liquid black
those pupils
of a bus kid
staring, staring
on his mother's lap

"Sanford Goldstein is known worldwide for his emotionally robust tanka, written in his distinctive "spilling" style. This collection of shorter poems at the "minimalist" end of the spectrum demonstrate his ability to surprise and delight us from inside what may appear to be another persona, but what is in fact classic Goldstein in timbre of voice, subject matter, and resilient spirit. His achievements in English-language tanka claim yet another territory. These poems are variously mobile and pungent, light and arrow-swift, and a joy to have at this juncture in a long, productive career."

Michael McClintock
President and co-founder, United Haiku and Tanka Society;
Lead editor, *The Tanka Anthology* (Red Moon Press, 2003)

"The book's title, *This Short Life,* is a reference not just to how short his long life seems, but how his life has been filled with short poetry. Goldstein, of course, is one of tanka's greatest masters in English, and these minimalist tanka show one of the reasons why. Treat yourself to these revealing poems by reading them slowly."

Michael Dylan Welch
Tanka Society of America founder

*This Short Life : Minimalist Tanka*
by Sanford Goldstein
Edited by M. Kei
ISBN-13: 978-1494845599 (Print) 164 pp
$15.00 USD / £ 9.00 GBP / € 11.00 EUR
$5.00 USD (Kindle)

Purchase in print at: https://www.createspace.com/4595498

* * *

# The Atomic Era - Call for Submissions

Submit to Don Miller: dmiller.u235@gmail.com

Reading Period: 1 March–30 April, 2015

July 16, 1945 marked the beginning of the Atomic Era. Though research and in-lab testing had been taking place prior to this date, the first test detonation of an atomic bomb occurred at the Trinity site in New Mexico, USA on this date. Three weeks later on August 6, 1945 this power became the greatest weapon of mass destruction when it was dropped on the unsuspecting city of Hiroshima, Japan. The mass destruction of this weapon was duplicated three days later on the city of Nagasaki, Japan. While these two dates are the only confirmed war time uses of an atomic weapon, unconfirmed reports exist of the USA using "tactical nuclear weapons" in their recent wars in Afghanistan and Iraq.

The irony of the atomic era is Japan now has some 50 nuclear power plants, and approximately 25 percent of Hiroshima's electricity and approximately 50 percent of Nagasaki's electricity is generated from nuclear power. However, since the events on March 11, 2011 resulting in the Fukushima Nuclear Power Plant disaster, all of Japan's nuclear power plants have reportedly been taken off-line. The last shutdown occurred on September 16, 2013. Though we know the dangers of nuclear power, without it we will utilize more coal and oil in the process of generating electricity, and the increased emissions from that process will increase the threat of global warming. So, will it be global warming or global nuclear radiation in answer to our energy needs?

By the time this Special Feature is published we will be into the 70th year of the atomic era, and a large majority of us have lived our entire lives since that date. That said, I am looking for high quality tanka on the topic of "The Atomic Era", whether it be on nuclear proliferation, nuclear disarmament, nuclear energy, or nuclear technology. Most of us are aware of the negatives associated with the atomic era; the challenge may be to write about the positives of nuclear technology. I would like to present a sampling of both the positive and negative aspects of the atomic era.

Tanka Submissions: Individuals are invited to submit up to five tanka poems each; however, no more than one poem will be selected from an individual poet in keeping with the theme and format of the '25 Poems' features on the Atlas Poetica website. Tanka submissions must be placed within the body of an email. No attached submissions will be opened.

Please submit your atomic/nuclear tanka to dmiller.u235@gmail.com with the subject line Atomic Era Tanka. Poems along with a brief bio (150 words or less) should be contained in the body of your email. Also include your name and Country. All submissions must be original and not previously published. Poems posted on social media are not eligible. All poems and bios in a language other than English, must be translated to English prior to submission. Please submit original language as well.

# BIOGRAPHIES

Alex von Vaupel lives in Utrecht, Netherlands, with his many dictionaries and a balcony vegetable garden. His tanka appear in *Atlas Poetica, Concise Delight, Prune Juice, Tanka Splendor, Take Five: Best Contemporary Tanka* (anthologies of 2009, 2010, 2011), and *Bright Stars*.

Ana Prundaru, a native Romanian, grew up in Japan and all over Western Europe. Currently she lives in Switzerland, where she works as an independent translator for small businesses and charities. Her work has appeared in *Halcyon Magazine, Cattails,* and *Gems,* an anthology of haiku by the Bamboo Hut Press, among others.

Anupam Sharma loves to write poetry and has keen interest in the Japanese forms. He has completed his graduation in Chemical Engineering this year, and believes that brevity has maximum potency to capture a snapshot.

Aruna Rao is primarily trained in the Visual Arts. Her love for anime led her to haiku and tanka which help her give shape to moments. Her tanka have been published in the *Undertow Tanka Review*, and Atlas Poetica Special Feature (India). She won an honourable mention in the UHTS Fleeting Words tanka contest 2014. Her works have also been selected for *A Hundred Gourds, Ribbons* and *moongarlic.*

Asni Amin is from Singapore. She stumbled upon haiku in early 2012 and has not stopped since then. Some of her haiku have been published in *Simply Haiku, a couple of tanka in Moonbathing Journal,* a few haiga in *The Daily Haiga,* etc. She also keeps a haiku blog "A Walk In Haiku." Asni won first place in the Second Edition Haiku Contest organised by the Romanian Kukai Group, Sharpening The Green Pencil in April 2013.

Autumn Noelle Hall makes her home in Green Mountain Falls, Colorado, USA, with her husband, two daughters, and one rapscallion Australian Shepherd. When not feeding the birds or photographing the mountains, she writes. Her poems provide temporary shelter for all the vagabond words drifting in her head. She is grateful to the many journals which have offered them more permanent quarters, and to you—their readers—who take the time to come by for a visit.

Barbara Taylor "Each day demands that I write and that my fingers touch and feel the earth." Her free verse poems, renku, haiga, haibun, haiku, tanka, and other Japanese short form poetry appear in international journals and anthologies on line and in print. She lives in the Rainbow Region, Northern NSW, Australia. Her diverse poems with audio are at http://batsword.tripod.com and more recently, at http://batsword.webs.com

Brian Zimmer lives in St. Louis, Missouri, within walking distance of the great Mississippi River. His work has appeared in various publications & journals both online and in print, including *Modern Tanka Today, red lights, The Tanka Journal* (Japan), *Gusts* & *Skylark*. He has been writing both micro and longer poetry for over forty years, devoting most of his efforts today to tanka and other Japanese short-forms.

Bruce England lives and works in Silicon Valley. His serious tanka writing began in 2010. Other related interests include haiku theory and practice. Long ago, a chapbook, *Shorelines*, was published with a friend, Tony Mariano.

Charles D. Tarlton is a retired university professor from New York now living in San Francisco with his wife, Ann Knickerbocker, a painter. He calls himself a poet (although this is a term Buckminster Fuller argued could not be self-ascribed) and has written poems all his life. He has been interested in and writing tanka prose since 2010.

Chen-ou Liu lives in Ajax, Ontario, Canada. He is the author of four books, including *Following the Moon to the Maple Land* (First Prize Winner of the 2011 Haiku Pix Chapbook Contest). His tanka and haiku have been honored with many awards.

David Rice has been writing tanka since 1990. He is the current editor of the Tanka Society of America's tri-annual journal, *Ribbons*. He lives in Berkeley, California.

Debbie Strange is a member of the Writers' Collective of Manitoba, as well as belonging to several haiku and tanka organizations. Her writing has received awards, and has been published in numerous journals. Debbie is also a singer/songwriter and an avid photographer. Her photographs have been published, and were recently featured in an abstract exhibition. Debbie is currently working on a haiga/tankart collection. She invites you to visit her on Twitter @Debbie_Strange.

Ernesto P. Santiago enjoys exploring the poetic myth of his senses, and has recently become interested in the study of haiku and its related forms. He is Filipino and lives in Athens, Greece.

Genie Nakano has an MFA in Dance from UCLA. She performs, choreographs dance and teaches Gentle Yoga, Meditation and Tanoshii Tanka at the Japanese Cultural Center in Gardena, CA. She was a journalist for the Gardena Valley Newspaper before she discovered tanka and haibun and was hooked. She enjoys performing the spoken work with music and movement/dance at open mics and cultural events.

Gerry Jacobson lived in Malaysia in the1960s. An experience which changed him profoundly. He now lives in Canberra, Australia, where he writes tanka and practises yoga.

Grunge is a gay Indo-American, who specialises in urban tanka. He currently lives in South Florida with a collection of pet arthropods, two cats, and an angry gecko.

Hannah Paul, poet from Pakistan
Sibling of no one
Scared of birds, but
Doesn't mind flying
Poems in books by Fraydtag. Pub
Haunts Twitter as @allthingspoetic

Hema Ravi has had a stint in the Central Government, then as a school teacher. Currently, she freelances as English Language Trainer. Her writeups have won prizes in the *Femina*, Khaleej Times (Dubai) and International Indian, Viewpoints been published in *The Hindu's Voice Your Views*. Prize winner in writersglobe.com. Prize Winner in Metverse Muse. Has published in *World Renewal Magazine*, *The Hans India Daily*, *Metverse Muse*, *Poetry World*, *Contemporary Literary Review Online and Print Edition*, *The Poetic Bliss*, *Roots and Wings* (An Anthology of Indian Women Writing in English), *The Fancy Realm*, *Matruvani* and *Holistic Mediscan*.

Jade Pandora resides in California, and was the 2010 recipient of the Matthew Rocca Poetry Award, Deakin University, Melbourne, Australia. She has studied and written Japanese short form poetry since 2007. A published poet, Jade can be found online at deviantART.

Janet Qually enjoys writing fiction, nonfiction, and many forms of poetry. She illustrates much of her work with computer graphics. Her short forms have appeared in *American Tanka* and *Ribbons*. In addition, a haibun is scheduled for the June 2014 issue of *Haibun Today*. Janet lives in Memphis, Tennessee.

Joann Grisetti grew up in Sasebo, Japan. She currently lives in Florida with her husband and two sons. Her poetry has appeared or is forthcoming in *Haiku Magazine*, *Daily Love*, *Lynx*, *Inclement*, *Poetry Quarterly*, *Atlas Poetica*, *Living Haiku Anthology*, *Autumn Legends*, *Whispers In The Wind*, *Haiku Journal*, *Wilderness House Review*, *Bright Stars*, and *Red Lights*. In addition, Joann has published short stories in the Inwood Indiana Press.

Joanna Ashwell, from County Durham, North East of England, member of the British Haiku Society, one haiku collection published by Hub Editions – 'Between Moonlight; published in *Presence*, *Blithe Spirit*, *Haibun Online* and various other publications.

John Tehan, currently of Cape Cod, Massachusetts, lived for many years in New York City where he enjoyed knowing many Indian and other South Asian men in a variety of contexts.

Julie B. Cain lives on a two-acre garden outside Sturgis, Mississippi (USA). She graduated with honors from Metropolitan State University of Denver with a major in Psychology and minor in Communication. She has traveled extensively and currently owns her own housekeeping business. She is also a professional portrait artist and muralist. She joined AHA Poetry Forum in 2009 and continues as a strong presence there. She has published in several tanka and haiku journals, among them: *AHA The Anthology*, *Notes From the Gean*, *A Hundred Gourds*, *Ribbons*, *Moonbathing* and has won an Honorable Mention in the Vancouver Cherry Blossom Festival.

Kala Ramesh. On the Board of Editors of Modern English Tanka Press's anthology, *Take Five: The Best Contemporary Tanka* for the years 2009/2010/2011, she has more than a 1000 poems comprising haiku, senryu, tanka, kyoka, haibun, tanka prose and renku, published in reputed journals and anthologies, both online and print editions in Japan, Europe, United Kingdom, Australia, United States of America and India. Kala is presently the Modern Haiku Editor for *Under the Basho* & the Editor of Youth

Corner, *Cattails* (UHTS). Kala is the external faculty member of Symbiosis International University, where she conducts a 60-hour module on haiku and allied genres like senryu, tanka, haibun, renku and haiga.

Kath Abela Wilson is the creator and leader of Poets on Site in Pasadena, California. Closely related to poetry of place, this group performs on the sites of their common inspiration. She loves the vitality and experimental micropoetic qualities of Twitter (@kathabela) and publishes in many print and online journals, as well as anthologies by Poets on Site.

M. Kei is the editor of *Atlas Poetica* and editor-in-chief of *Take Five : Best Contemporary Tanka*. He is a tall ship sailor in real life and has published nautical novels featuring a gay protagonist, *Pirates of the Narrow Seas*. His most recent novel is an Asian-themed science fiction/fantasy novel, *Fire Dragon*.

Mariko Kitakubo was born in Tokyo. She is a member of the Tanka Society of America, Association of Contemporary Tanka Poets, Kokoro no Hana, Japan PEN Club, Japan Tanka Poets Club, Tanka Online project <http://tanka.kitakubo.com / english>. Mariko has published five books of tanka including two bilingual ones, "On This Same Star" and "Cicada Forest." She has also produced a CD of her tanka titled "Messages." Mariko is an experienced performer who has presented her poetry on at least 108 occasions, 58 of them overseas. She hopes by this to encourage more poetry lovers worldwide to appreciate and practice tanka.

Marilyn Humbert lives in the outer Northern suburbs of Sydney surrounded by bush. Her work appears in *Eucalypt, Kokako, Moonbathing, Simply Haiku* and *Atlas Poetica*.

Michael G. Smith lives in Santa Fe, NM. His poetry has been published or is forthcoming in *Atlas Poetica, Borderlands: Texas Poetry Review, Cider Press Review, Nimrod, Sulphur River Literary Review, the Kerf, The Santa Fe Literary Review* and other journals. *The Dark is Different in Reverse*, a chapbook, was published by Bitterzoet Press in 2013. *No Small Things*, a full-length book of poetry, was published by Tres Chicas Books in 2014.

Natsuko Wilson lives in Ontario and has enjoyed going to Cape Cod for summer over thirty years. Trained as a musician, she tries to weave music and photography into tanka.

Nicholas B. Hamlin is a poet, lyricist, song-writer and coffee roaster living in South Pasadena, CA. He is 23.

Nilufer Y. Mistry was born and brought up in Calcutta, India. She now resides in British Columbia, Canada, along with her family. She is an artist. She discovered micropoetry on Twitter in 2011 and is an avid member of this virtual community ever since @NiluferYM. Her micropoems usually reflect Nature but also document everyday-life, as they unfold around her.

Patricia Prime is co-editor of the New Zealand haiku magazine, *Kokako*, reviews/interviews editor of *Haibun Today*, and is a reviewer for *Takahe* and *Atlas Poetica*, and for several Indian magazines. She has interviewed poets and editors for *Takahe* and for the online magazines *Haiku NewZ, Simply Haiku, Haibun Today, Stylus*. She co-edited, with Australian poets, Amelia Fielden and Beverley George, the tanka collection *100 Tanka by 100 Poets* and is currently editing, with Dr. Bruce Ross and others, the world haiku anthology *A Vast Sky*. Patricia writes haiku, tanka, haibun and tanka prose and has published her poetry worldwide.

Pavithra Satheeshkumar received BA and MA in English Literature from University of Bangalore and MPhil in English Literature from University of Mysore. She is active in all forms of creative writing, translation, and literary criticism. Her works have appeared in journals like *The Criterion, Red Fez, East Coast Literary Review* and *Panju*. Born and raised in India, she now lives in Waco, Texas, USA.

Payal A. Agarwal is a poet residing in India who likes to play around with words. A few of his works are forthcoming, both online and in print.

Peter Fiore lives and writes in Mahopac, New York, USA. His poems have been published in *American Poetry Review, Poetry Now, Atlas Poetica, red lights, A Hundred Gourds,* and *Bright Stars* among others. In 2009, Peter published *text messages* the first volume of American poetry totally devoted to Gogyohka.

Pravat Kumar Padhy, Scientist and Poet. His haiku, tanka and haibun have appeared in *The World Haiku Review, Lynx, Four and Twenty, The Notes from the Gean, Atlas Poetica, Simply Haiku, Red lights, Ribbons, The Heron's Nest, Inner Art Journal, Shamrock, A Hundred Gourds, Vancouver Cherry Blossom Festival, Magnapoets, Bottle Rockets, Mu International, Frogpond, Kokako, Presence, Issa's Untidy Hut, The Bamboo Hut*, etc. Recently his tanka have been anthologized in *Fire Pearls 2* and *Bright Stars*, edited by M Kei.

Radhey Shiam was born on Jan. 14, 1922, and inherited a love for literature, influenced by Mr. Alfred

Emanuel Sorensen and American artist-*cum*-philosopher Mr. E. Brewster, both friends to Pt. Jawahar Lal Nehru. Contributor to the *First Hindu Haiku Anthology* (India 1989), *First Hay (Na)ku Anthology* (USA 2005), and several anthologies in Hindi. He pioneered haiku songs *Haiku Riddles* and *Haiku Ghazals*. His haiku and tanka have appeared in *World Haiku Club Showcase, Moonset, Modern English Tanka, Among the Lilies,* etc. Award Honarable Mention—The Saigyo Award for Tanka 2009. Revista Haiku Acorda Diploma—Award May, 2014, The Japanese Tanka Poets Society 2009. Publication—'Song of Life' published by Bhartiya Vidya Bhawa.

Ram Krishna Singh, born, brought up and educated in Varanasi (Uttar Pradesh, India), has been writing haiku and tanka for the last three decades. His published volumes include *Above the Earth's Green* (1997), *Every Stone Drop Pebbles* (jointly with Catherine Mair and Patricia Prime, 1999), *Pacem in Terris* (jointly with Myriam Pierri and Giovanni, 2003), *The River Returns: A Collection of Tanka and Haiku* (2006), *Sexless Solitude and Other Poems* (2009), *Sense and Silence: Collected Poems* (2010) and *New and Selected Poems Tanka and Haiku* (2012). A professor of English, he has been teaching language skills to students of earth and mineral sciences at Indian School of Mines, Dhanbad (India) since 1976.

Rebecca Drouilhet is a 59 year-old retired registered nurse. Her haiku and tanka have been published in numerous print and e-journals. She enjoys playing word games and spending time with her large family in Picayune, Mississippi.

Richard St. Clair (b. 1946) has only visited India in his imagination. Raised in North Dakota (USA), he is a prolific composer of modern classical music and a retired concert pianist with a doctoral degree in music from Harvard University. He has written haiku for over 20 years and tanka for 15 years. Recently he set English tanka of Jun Fujita to music. His own tanka have appeared elsewhere in *Atlas Poetica* and *Bright Stars.* A Jodo Shinshu Buddhist, he currently resides in Cambridge, Massachusetts.

Rodney Williams' poetry in Japanese short-forms has been widely published internationally across an extended period. In 2012, he edited "Snipe Rising From A Marsh – Birds in Tanka" as a Special Feature for Atlas Poetica online. His book *A bird-loving man: haiku and tanka* was published by Ginninderra Press in 2013. This year he has been appointed Secretary of the Australian Haiku Society (working through the HaikuOz website).

Samantha Sirimanne Hyde was born in Sri Lanka and now lives in Australia. She is grateful to have recently crossed paths with the exquisite world of haiku, tanka, and other Japanese poetry forms.

Sanford Goldstein has been writing tanka for more than fifty years. In addition, he has co-translated many Japanese writers—those in poetry, to cite a few, are Akiko Yosano, Mokichi Saitō, Shiki Masaoka, and Takuboku Ishikawa. It is to Takuboku that Goldstein feels most indebted. Takuboku believed that tanka is a poem involving the emotional life of the poet. Goldstein's poems focus on what he has experienced, suddenly seen, suddenly reflected on—they are not imagined.

Sonam Chhoki was born and raised in the eastern Himalayan kingdom of Bhutan. She has been writing Japanese short forms of haiku, tanka and haibun for about 5 years. These forms resonate with her Tibetan Buddhist upbringing and provide the perfect medium for the exploration of her country's rich ritual, social and cultural heritage. She is inspired by her father, Sonam Gyamtsho, the architect of Bhutan's non-monastic modern education. Her works have been published in poetry journals and anthologies in Australia, Canada, Japan, UK and US and included in the Cultural Olympics 2012 Poetry Parnassus and BBC Radio Scotland Written Word programme.

toki is a published poet and recent addition to the Keibooks editorial team. Born and raised in the Pacific Northwest US, toki often writes poetry informed by the experience of that region: the labyrinthine confines of the evergreen forests, the infinite vastness of the sea and inclement sky, and the liminal spaces in between. toki's poetry can be found online and in print, with work published in *Atlas Poetica, The Bamboo Hut,* and *Poetry Nook.*

Yancy Carpentier is a student of the 18th & 19th centuries. Her interests include military and maritime history, and poetry of all flavors. The Mediterranean and the Ottoman Empire are her keenest attractions. Previously administrative assistant to a feisty group of cardiologists, she catered to their whims, steered them straight, and tried to keep them humble. Her professional life over at last, she loves to read and garden. Yancy lives in the Deep South with her best friend/husband.

# INDEX

Our 'butterfly' is actually an Atlas moth (Attacus atlas), the largest butterfly/moth in the world. It comes from the tropical regions of Asia. Image from the 1921 *Les insectes agricoles d'époque*.

## Publications by Keibooks

*Atlas Poetica : A Journal of Poetry of Place in Contemporary Tanka*

## Collections Edited by M. Kei

*circling smoke, scattered bones,* by Joy McCall

*Hedgerows, Tanka Pentaptychs,* by Joy McCall

*This Short Life, Minimalist Tanka,* by Sanford Goldstein

## Anthologies Edited by M. Kei

*Bright Stars, An Organic Tanka Anthology (Vols. 1–6)*

*Take Five : Best Contemporary Tanka (Vol. 4)*

## M. Kei's Poetry Collections

*January, A Tanka Diary*

*Slow Motion : The Log of a Chesapeake Bay Skipjack*
tanka and short forms

*Heron Sea : Short Poems of the Chesapeake Bay*
tanka and short forms

## M. Kei's Novels

*Pirates of the Narrow Seas 1 : The Sallee Rovers*
*Pirates of the Narrow Seas 2 : Men of Honor*
*Pirates of the Narrow Seas 3 : Iron Men*
*Pirates of the Narrow Seas 4 : Heart of Oak*

*Man in the Crescent Moon : A Pirates of the Narrow Seas Adventure*
*The Sea Leopard : A Pirates of the Narrow Seas Adventure*

*Fire Dragon*